ESSENTIAL SOFTWARE
TEST DESIGN

BY TORBJÖRN RYBER

ESSENTIAL SOFTWARE TEST DESIGN

TEST DESIGN

BY TORBJÖRN RYBER

FEARLESS
CONSULTING

Copyright © Fearless Consulting KB
A Production with Unique Publishing Ltd
English translation by Philip Meddings, Estilo Translations
Cover Art & design Alexandra Németh, Grundform
Illustrations Alexandra Németh, Grundform
Production Manager Cecilia Henricson
Typographer Elisabet Jensen
Printed Mediaprint Uddevalla AB, Sverige 2007

ISBN 13: 978-91-85699-03-2
ISBN 10: 91-85699-03-9

Dedication:
For Karin, Elin and Alice

CONTENT

PART II

PART III

FOREWORD: BY JAMES BACH

TORBJÖRN RYBER HAS a problem: He has testing skill, and he wants to share that skill with you, but this is very hard to do with a book. What he can do with a book is name and describe ideas that live in his head, hoping that those words will trigger or amplify insights and experiences that «already» live in your head and manifest in your experiences. He can point toward testing and say «there!» but you have to look beyond the end of his finger to understand what he's trying to say.

Part of how Torbjörn tries to solve this problem is to offer you heuristics. A heuristic is a fallible method of solving a problem or making a decision. The key idea of heuristics is that they can be useful even though they aren't «guaranteed» to be useful. That means the responsibility to understand and apply this material effectively lies with you. Do not just copy or memorize the test ideas in this book. Instead, do what Torbjörn and I do: take the ideas in, try to understand the underlying point, argue with them a bit, and try applying the part that makes sense. (And even this advice is heuristic.)

Let me illustrate. In his section on equivalence class partitioning, Torbjörn tells us that «The idea is that, if you expect the same result from two tests, it is sufficient to run one of them.» This may seem like a strange thing to say, because if you really think about it:

– Isn't the whole point of testing to see whether our expectations are fulfilled or violated? If it's okay to claim we know what the result of a test would be without even running it, then why not do that for all tests? We would end up running no tests and all and be finished testing very quickly.

– Sometimes doing the «same» action many times will result in a failure on the Nth attempt. If your goal is to find every bug, running duplicate tests many times may be an important idea. Certainly tests that are slightly different would have an even greater chance of finding a bug.

– What is and isn't the «same» is impossible for us to say with certainty, but however we determine this, it will depend on how we model the system. If I test 2+2 on a calculator, do I also need to try $(34+56+10)*10-996$? By looking at the steps, the two tests seem very different, but if we just look at the final expected result, they appear to be the same.

I think what Torbjörn is trying to get across is that we can't do every possible different test based on every possible different way of modeling the system, so as a heuristic we may prefer to run tests that are more different instead of tests that are more the same. Variety is the spice of testing! In the examples of equivalence classes that he provides, he's expressing his sense of which differences may not matter much, in some contexts (while in other contexts those differences may matter a lot). Your task is not to memorize his choices, but to look at your own product and make your own choices based on your own evolving knowledge of the technology.

That brings us to test design. This book focuses on test design, and I'm glad that it does. Design is the intellectual part of testing. It's the puzzle solving part. And design is a heuristic process. There is no formula you apply, no crank you can turn, to produce good tests. Don't look for those kinds of answers, here. What you will see are suggestions and demonstrations. As Torbjörn explains, what you're doing when you test is modeling the product in various ways and then covering those models, in a useful and economical way, with your clever test designs. This is a skill, and though Torbjörn can't directly give you that skill through a book, this book will provide clues for developing it.

James Bach

FOREWORD: BY STUART REID

I VIEW TEST case design as *the* core skill of the software testing discipline. Partly this is because it was the first skill I attempted to master as a software tester. However, even now, when I would argue that the majority of software testing problems stem from poor test management, for me it is still the fundamental building block of the software test professional. The special challenge of selecting a test set that is a useful, but relatively tiny sample from the practically infinite set of possible test inputs defines the testing discipline and continues to intrigue me.

This book, Essential Test Design, is aptly named. There are already several well-respected and useful books on designing test cases that I couldn't do without. However, in this book Torbjörn Ryber has managed to produce a text that is not only useful, but also concise and to-the-point. Despite being kept to a sensible length it still manages to include guest chapters and material from renowned experts in areas such as combinatorial testing and exploratory testing, and understanding is greatly enhanced by the widespread use of examples that clearly demonstrate the application of the techniques.

Unlike many texts on test design it is not purely aligned with a scripted approach to software testing, but instead declares itself as part of the context-driven school. It thus opens up the possibility of the described techniques being used across the whole range of testing approaches, from highly-scripted at one extreme to exploratory at the other.

Born out of Torbjörn's popular courses on test design, this book offers a perfect introduction to the topic. This makes it an obvious selection to accompany such courses, as well as providing an excellent ongoing reference for software test analysts and managers alike.

Stuart Reid

PREFACE BY AUTHOR

MORE THAN A year has passed since the original version was published in Swedish. The contents are very similar in this English version so you might find some comments that are intended especially for a Swedish audience but I am sure you will see that as a nice local touch.

Mats Grindal has written a new chapter on combinatorial testing based on his recent doctoral thesis on the subject. This is a great enhancement from the earlier chapter that was limited to pair-wise testing.

I believe that testing is context-driven. This means that that there are no best practices only good practices in context. In every job I do I have to adapt what I know to fit the given situation, this also applies to the techniques I know and teach as well as to any templates that I present in the book.

This book is based mainly on my own personal experiences and to some extent on the observations of colleagues. The emphasis is put on presenting to you a number of useful techniques which adapted to each individual situation have worked well in a number of projects. I do not in any way claim that this book is exhaustive or that it is a perfect fit for you. But these are the lessons I wish I had been given at the start of my testing career some twelve years back.

A survey was recently conducted on how twelve companies that develop software, some of it safety-critical, use test design in their organisations. Of the twelve, only three of them used any structured approach at all and they mainly used equivalence partitioning and boundary value analysis. I was shocked at their ignorance. I do not consider it important for all of us testers to have a tool box of test design techniques rather it is essential! There is no place for sloppy testing in the future! So if you start reading the rest of this book I will try to calm down a bit. Enjoy!!

I give classes in test design on a regular basis. If you are interested in cooperating in any way or if you have any comments in general please contact me at torbjorn@ryber.se

Torbjörn Ryber

1 PREFACE

Every genuine test of a theory is an attempt to falsify it, or to refute it.

- KARL POPPER

ABSOLUTELY THE MOST important factor for success in testing is good test design. It does not matter how nice-looking your documents are, or how good your plans are, if the tests do not measure up. In principle, this whole book is about simplifying a complicated reality into manageable models, and from these, choosing the right type of test cases from among the variations available. There is a clear advantage to be gained in making use of systematic techniques for creating more variants on test cases more effectively.

I have worked in testing within many different sectors, from giants of telecommunications, banking, insurance and the public sector, to powerful but small internet companies. I have also read a great deal of written material on the subject. Although there are many books about testing, most of them lack any decent description of the very nucleus of work in testing, namely effective test design. A lot of what is written about testing is relatively generic and focuses on processes, how to manage the work, and which documents are to be produced. If we delete all these aspects from the picture, we are left with the question of what testing actually is. How do I go about it? This book deals with these questions in detail.

There are a great many standards and accreditations within testing but none of them owe their strength to test design. Depending on whom you ask, you will get different replies to the question of what is the most important thing to be able to do. I have tried to bring together those techniques that are most useful when you are trying to do a good job as a test designer. In my world a test designer is responsible for analysing and challenging the test basis at hand, and then creating test cases for checking how well the software is functioning compared to the requirements on it. The term test analyst is also sometimes used for this role.

Development in IT is proceeding at a breathtaking pace. Ever more advanced systems are being built in an ever shorter time, and the requirements on them are such that they have to work faultlessly, and work 24 hours a day. What previously could probably be dealt with through hard work, now requires a more methodical approach. In order to be able to carry out better testing in a shorter time, you have to work smarter than before. The key is to tackle the problem in a structured way with the help of a toolbox loaded with modelling skills and test techniques. If you master many different techniques, and know when to use them, you have a significantly better chance of doing a good job.

I strongly believe that in the future, there will be no place for testers who lack a high level of competence in test design. Other important areas to be mastered are programming and automation. The material in this book has been developed over many years, and is built on actual experiences, mostly my own. The aim is to provide instruction as to those techniques that are the most important for your success in the test design aspect of your projects.

1.1   Whom the Book is Intended For

This book is intended, first and foremost, for all those who work in some form of testing or development of systems where software is present. Regardless of whether you are working as a developer, or as a tester, the ideas and techniques are general, and are suited to both problems of a more technical character as well as overarching business processes.

The content is based on course material which has been compiled over many years, and also contains references to books and articles that have been used as source material. The book is therefore quite suitable, both as a basis for academic teaching, and for self-tuition.

1.2   The Structure of the Book

Part I: These introductory chapters are here to provide you with overarching information about what testing is. They contain reflections about how testing is influenced by different development models, and about different types of approach.

Part II: This is the main body of the book, and deals with how to produce good test cases effectively. The test design techniques described are all usable in practice, and complement each other. The theories behind the techniques are described thoroughly, and each technique is demonstrated with the help of examples that you can follow step by step. The most important ones also include exercises. Being able to use the techniques is the first step: knowing how to adapt them to your particular project is a skill which will come the more you work with them.

You will often end up in situations where you have to adapt the techniques described, or use other techniques in order to solve your problems. You are welcome to share these experiences with the author for future editions of this book.

Part III: The final part deals with practical details about how to organise your test cases, how to carry out tests and deal with defects. There are also tips for further reading, both on testing and on other interesting related subjects.

1.3   What is not in This Book

Ideas about how to manage test projects, how to improve your test process or general information about quality control work lies outside the scope of this book.

Static testing is only dealt with in summary. Non-functional testing and tools lie outside the scope of this book.

To learn about the general ideas behind testing it is recommended, either that you undergo an elementary course in test methodology or read one of the books written on the subject. See the list of suggested reading.

1.4   The Author

Torbjörn Ryber is a true test enthusiast and a popular speaker at conferences. He has spoken about test to several thousand people. This book is the result of many years of teaching test design with the goal of giving the students more material to bring home than just the regular stack of slide-copies that resides safely on a shelf until finally recycled. Torbjörn has a Master of Science degree in Computer Science and has been working since 1995 on requirements management and testing in the development of computer systems. He has spent five years on the board of the Swedish Association for Software Testing (SAST), three of them as chairman.

1.5   Acknowledgements

Many people have been involved, both in producing and scrutinising the content of this book. Many thanks to:

Carl-Johan Nordh at KnowIT who has always encouraged me and who has sponsored a large part of this translations to English.

My panel of experts and other guest reviewers: Ann-Charlotte Bolander, Hans Engberg, Lillemor Ehrner, Jesper Hansén, Dan Hernvall, Hans Larsson, Hans-Gunnar Leytman, Sofie Nordhamrén, Mattias Nordin, Ingvar Nordström, Peter Ohlsson and Gun Ström. Without your points of view, this book would not have become what it has become.

Reviewers of the English version Stuart Reid,

Peter Zimmerer, Harry Robinson and Vipul Kocher, for allowing me to use parts of their own material in this book. Cem Kaner, Rex Black, Michael Bolton and everyone else in the Software Testing discussion group, for their ideas and answers to my questions.

Thanks to Mats Grindal who wrote the chapter on combinatorial testing that has replaced the chapter on pair-wise testing.

A special word of thanks to James Bach for the chapter on *Exploratory*

Testing and for reviewing the compilation of this book. He is also an inspiration for us rapidly progressing testers, through challenging what we believe we already know. Many of the ideas in this book have been inspired by James.

PART I

THESE INTRODUCTORY CHAPTERS are here to provide you with overarching information about what testing is. They contain reflections about how testing is influenced by different development models, and about different types of approach to testing.

2 INTRODUCTION

The criterion of the scientific status of a theory is its... testability
                                                    - KARL POPPER

AS A TESTER, you are faced, on a daily basis, with a host of different problems. The requirements profile is incomplete and changes over time, systems are getting ever more complex and, at the same time, the production of new software is meant to be getting faster. How do we solve this? There are a number of good elementary ideas for how you can succeed in testing.[1]

2.1   Insufficient Requirements

As a basis for all system development, there is often some documentation in the form of requirements. A common problem is that the requirements in existence are not a good enough basis for constructing our tests. I would go so far as to say that, in reality, it is impossible to obtain a perfect requirements specification. It is important, therefore, for a test designer to be involved in the project early on and to have views about the content and testability of those requirements.

Testability for requirements involves them having to be:
• clear: that it should be unequivocally clear what the requirements involve
• compatible with each other: that different requirements do not contradict each other
• complete: the requirements at hand describe the whole picture
• measurable: we should be able to generate test cases for them

Our aim as testers is to run a number of test cases, and from the result of these tests, tell whether the requirements appear to be met or not.

Examining documentation from top to bottom by some kind of formal method, such as inspection, can eliminate many defects. Certainly, more informal walkthroughs of the documentation are common, and show up the severest defects, but in my experience, there are few who review in an effective way since this requires a lot of time, and good practices.

An effective alternative to obtaining testable requirements is to study all the basic information you can find and then build models which describe the requirements, for example matrices, diagrams, graphs and flow diagrams. According to development processes like RUP, this should be done by a requirements analyst, but the fact is that, many times, it is the testers who have to do the job when the requirements land on their lap. From the models, we can then ask questions like, «From what you have written/said, do I take it that this is how it should work? Does this correspond with your understanding?» This works infinitely better than simply protesting that the test basis are insufficient. When there are changes in the requirements, it is relatively easy for us to see how it affects our models, and then arrive at how we must adapt the test cases.

If the situation is really bad, and the requirement documentation is completely missing, it is difficult to carry out really good tests. In these cases, test design work will largely be working on the requirements themselves, with the models and the complete test cases constituting the whole set of requirements at the same time, one way or another. It can become a time-consuming thing to do, to arrange meetings where developers, those setting the requirements, and others work together to find answers to questions about how the system should work. You can test without any requirements, but the results will not be as good. Also, see the chapter on exploratory testing, where the most extreme case is where we do not have any written test procedures at all before we start carrying out the tests.

2.2 Infinite Number of Possible Test Cases

Even for a very small system or function, there are an infinite number of possible test cases. A function can most often be used in several different ways, with a combination of different input data and with other events taking place simultaneously in the system. For a tester, it is a case of finding out what combinations and events are most important to test.

A good test case has a good chance of finding a defect so far undiscovered. Since it is impossible to cover every different variant of events and data, it is a case of finding the set of conceivable test cases which have the greatest chance of detecting the most serious defects.[2]

It is a case of writing test cases both for valid and invalid events. Remember that there are often more ways of making a mistake than of performing a task correctly. The different techniques for test design are suited to different things. One single technique does not detect all types of defect – in every project, therefore, you have to use several different techniques.[3]

In principle, this entire book is about simplifying a complicated reality into manageable models, and from these choosing the right test case from among the variants available. You will probably recognise many of the techniques described – it is common for them to be used, even on an informal basis. There is a clear benefit to be gained from making use of formal techniques for finding more variants on a type of test more effectively.

2.3   Less Time

Boehm's classic model on how much it costs to detect defects at different points in time in the project forms a curve with the cost of correcting defects rising exponentially over time.[4] Cem Kaner writes, in a more exhaustive analysis, that it is expensive to change the requirements when the code has already been written, or to repair a product already sold to a client.[5] Even more recent assessments show that the cost of correcting defects, depending on what they are, can rise a hundredfold from the requirement stages to the point of production.[6] I accept these overarching results, but I believe that they present too much of a simplification to be of help to us.

There is no absolute truth about how much every individual defect costs to put right, and one problem in how Boehm's graph is presented is that it can be interpreted as though all defects must always be detected as early as possible. A more detailed analysis would suggest that you have to find the *right* type of defect at the *right* time. Defects involving the requirements or the design of the system should be detected before coding begins – that is unquestionable. These types of defect are expensive to correct late on in a project, when time has been spent specifying, coding, and testing the invalid design. Note that the agile alliance thinks differently on this matter. For this type of defect, Boehm's curve works well (*Boehm's graph is below.*) Certain types of coding defects should be detected and corrected by the developer, since this person can both test and correct the defect in a shorter time than anyone else, but they cannot be detected earlier when there is no code to test.

For certain simpler types of defects, it can be the case that the cost per defect stays the same right up to testing. (*Example 1 in the graph*) Besides this there are, in fact, certain types of defect that are both more difficult and expensive to detect early on in a project. Without having carried out any advanced research on the subject, I will stick my neck out and say that certain defects are both easier and cheaper to detect during system testing, than during component testing. This may be down to the fact that it is often extremely expensive to create a good environment in the early stages, or that we do not have the full picture early on in the development stage, or that simpler coding defects are relatively easy to correct even when they occur late on in the project. Moreover, it is we as testers who are the specialists and, therefore, we work more effectively on writing good test cases, compared with the developers. In the same way, it sometimes costs more to review the test cases carefully, than to analyse anomalous results after the test case has been carried out. Here is a simple example to illustrate this. In one project, I generated 120 test cases in the form of two files, with a total of 35,000 fields. Scrutinising all of these fields in order to make the test case completely defect-free would have taken me several days. Instead, we ran the test data through the program to be tested and found twelve defects that were test data dependent. Correction of the test data, plus the *retest* took us just two hours, significantly less time than an analysis would have taken. (*Example 2 in the graph*)

I am convinced that we must do the right thing at the right time, and so we can do a better job in less time! That sounds like a tale from Utopia but I know from my own experience that it works. Modelling and effective test design are two important steps along the road.

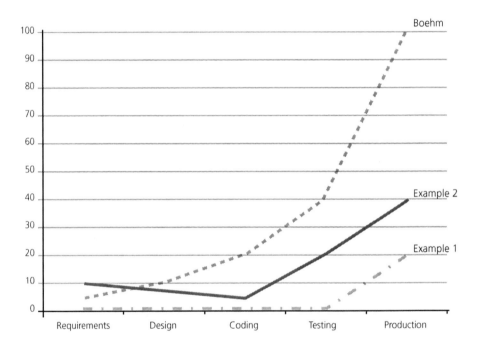

Figure 2.1: Cost of detecting and correcting defects at different stages in development. Boehm's classic curve shows that the cost of detecting and correcting mistakes rises exponentially over time. Other curves show how the cost can vary for specific types of defect.

2.4   Other Tips
Added to the points above, here are some useful tips for how to succeed as a test designer.

ESSENTIAL SOFTWARE TEST DESIGN

- Be flexible. Every project is unique and brings with it different challenges for you to solve, and skill in adapting your work to the situation in hand is essential.
- Make it your guiding star to add value to your project. Think about this before you do or say anything, and you will avoid making enemies. As a tester, you are often the bearer of bad news, so it is important for you to be both diplomatic and positive.
- Draw up a skills plan for yourself, so that you become more valuable. Besides raising your status and, hopefully, your salary, it is infinitely more fun working with testing, the better you are. Start by reading this book and practising on your projects... but do not stop there. There is a mass of written material, information on the web, conferences and courses available which is invaluable to your future.
- If you learn to model systems and functions, you will be able to analyse many demands, and then this knowledge becomes invaluable.

FOOTNOTES

[1]   In Sweden, we sometimes differentiate between the role of a test designer, who specialises in developing test cases, and that of test executors , who carry out the tests. The most common aspect of material from overseas is to use the term «tester» to indicate the person who deals both with the creation and the execution of test cases.

[2]   Myers, Glenford [1979] *The Art of Software Testing*, p.36

[3]   Beizer, Boris [1995], *Black Box Testing* p.11

[4]   Boehm, B W [1976]: *Software Engineering, IEEE Transactions on Computers*, C-25

[5]   Kaner, Cem, Jack Falk, Hung Nguyen[1999]: *Testing Computer Software* p.31

[6]   Wiegers, Karl [2003]: *Software Requirements*, p.17

3 WHAT IS TESTING?

TESTING IS TO ask questions of a test object and compare the answers with some kind of expected result in order to decide whether a particular aspect of the test object works as intended. Some have formulated it a little differently:

> Testing is the process of using a system or component under given circumstances, of observing or noting the results, and carrying out an evaluation of the system or component from a given perspective.[7]
>
> Testing is the process of executing a program with the purpose of detecting defects.[8]
>
> Testing is questioning a product in order to evaluate it.[9]

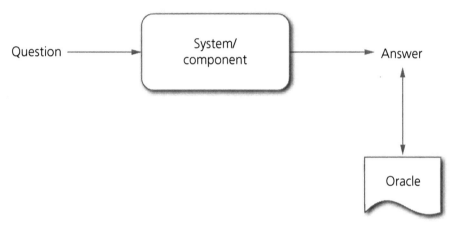

Figure 3.1: Testing is to ask questions and evaluate the answers against an oracle of some kind. All tests have four main problems: how do we ask the questions; what questions do we ask; how do we look at the answers and; what is our Oracle, i.e.where do we find our expected result?

The above picture speaks volumes about the challenges we face when working as testers. We have to know both how to *ask* questions and also to *know which* questions to ask. We must be able to interpret the answers and have something to compare them with. In more detailed tests, and in component testing, we even have to study what happens within the system. Testing can even be regarded as a way of measuring how far we have come in terms of development. Testability is the sum of all factors above.

Aside from the above definitions, there is Static Testing. This involves us researching and checking whether what is in place is correct, without executing any code. The techniques for this are entirely separate from the above descriptions and, although static techniques are counted as testing, according to most testing standards, all the listed definitions exclude this fact, which can be considered a little remarkable.

3.1   Controllability – How Do We Ask the Questions?

In certain cases, we can feed in data ourselves, as users, via a graphical or text-based interface. Here, we mostly use a keyboard and mouse, although there may be other ways of influencing the system, such as remote controls (TV, stereo), breath-input devices (alcohol lock) or push-buttons (traffic signals, lifts).

It is also common to use some type of file interface, whether predefined or generated just for testing. There is often even a programmable interface (API) which makes it possible to take advantage of functions within the program or in input modules, for certain available functions in another program or group of functions.

Practical problems we often come up against are that it is difficult to ask questions before the whole system is complete. Moreover, the interface which the end-user will end up with may turn out to be impractical or impossible to use for us to run the whole range of test scenarios we want to carry out.

If possible, we can require the system to be built with extra functionality for the purpose of carrying out tests – i.e. built-in testability. This means that controllability and observability of the system is increased which enables s to test faster and better.

3.2   Test Design – What Questions Do We Ask?

From the infinite number of questions it is a matter for us to make the right choice. We must choose the questions that are good enough and which, together, provide us with acceptable coverage. The hard part is determining what and how much is good enough! The more questions we manage to ask, the more we know about how well our system functions. The whole of this book is about precisely this problem, which we call test design.

3.3   Observability – How Do We See the Answers?

In the same way as we ask the questions, we can also get the answers via a graphical or text-based interface. It is also common for us to obtain a result file or a paper report and, sometimes, an audible signal or mechanical reaction, for example, from a mobile telephone, lift or microwave oven.

3.4 Oracle – How Do We Know if The Answers are Correct?

One of our problems lies in obtaining an expected result to compare with, and this is often called the Oracle problem. Depending on the type of test we carry out, there are different oracles to suit. Some of the most common are:

- An expected result described as a part of the requirements
- Manually calculated
- Calculations in some type of tool: e.g. MS Excel™
- Earlier versions of the same product: in those cases we perform an update of existing code
- Other similar products that we estimate are correct: e.g. internal or external systems with the same data or functions
- Completed suites of tests which somebody else has built and tested. This is often used for testing compilers, web browsers and SQL-tools[10]

3.4.1 Heuristics

James Bach provides what he calls heuristics for oracles, which are more general answers to the question of how a system should behave.[11] Below are some of the things to consider.

- Consistent with history and our image
- Consistent with similar products
- Consistent within product
- Consistent with user´s expectations

3.4.2 High Volume Automated Testing

When automated tests are carried out there are completely different oracles that apply. Harry Robinson, who is one of the leading experts on automated robustness testing, talks about running the system for a long period with masses of input data, and checking the following:[12]

- Unauthorised error messages should not appear – e.g. search for the text *Error*
- The system should not crash
- Features which lock up, where you stick in one place, should not be present

3.5 Example: Loan Application

We are going to test a system which handles applications for loans. From the user's point of view, the system consists of a GUI-dialogue, where particular details about the customer are fed in, for example, salary, while information about the customer's assets and current loans and any remarks are already in the dialogue. So, from a system-testing perspective, we both ask questions, and get answers, via a dialogue. However, we have another problem, namely that, because time is limited, we must also test the component handling the set of rules, before the dialogue is complete.

- Problem 1: Testing the set of rules before the dialogue is complete, since time is limited
- Problem 2: Partial results – is the test data being used correctly? (It is difficult to test the set of rules in detail without seeing the partial results)

Testing the set of rules component in advance naturally requires an interface for both questions and answers.

1. The test cases are written in a text file which has the same format as the *input area* that the set of rules component has. Thus, we pretend that the information comes from the dialogue.
2. Since we not only want the answer, but also to check that the input variables are being handled correctly, we ask for the partial results to be compiled through what we call a *display* being written to a file during the period that the set of rules is working- these are the temporary results.
3. We generate the test cases in an Excel spreadsheet where the set of rules is simulated. This template contains both the partial and final results.
4. Hand all test cases and the expected results over to the developer, who personally conducts an initial test.
5. In the analysis of our test results, we detect only a few defects. This I contribute to the fact that we have written the test cases early on, and given them to the developer, we have thus contributed to an improved component test.
6. The final step is testing the dialogue connected with the set of rules. Now, we know that the rules are being implemented correctly, and can focus on ensuring that the dialogue is sending the right data to the set of rules. As we had expected, we detect defects in the connection between the dialogue and the set of rules, but no new defects in the set of rules component itself.

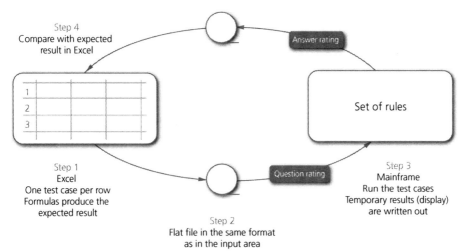

Figure 3.2: Strategy for testing the set of rules component separately. For this, we have to compile an interface for both questions and answers. The answer is compiled in an Excel template

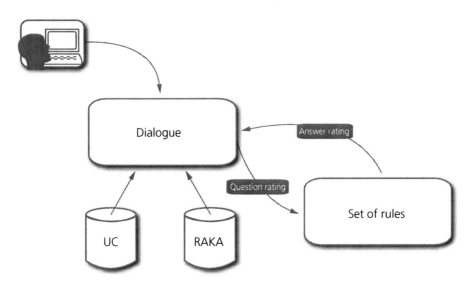

Figure 3.3: Testing the dialogue, connected to the set of rules. We use the dialogue's graphic interface for both questions and answers. The oracle is the same Excel sheet as before. Our focus is now on integration between the parts.

FOOTNOTES

7 *IEEE Standard* 610.12-1990

8 Myers, Glenford [1979] *The Art of Software Testing*, p.5

9 Bach, James [2005]: *Rapid Testing course material.*

10 Copeland, Lee [2003]: *A Practitioner's Guide to Software Test Design* pp. 6–7

11 Bach, James [2005]: *Rapid Testing course material.*

12 Robinson[2005]: *EuroSTAR Tutorial Model-Based Testing*

4 DEVELOPMENT MODELS

The quality of the testing process determines whether the test effort will be succesful. [13]

IN THE BEGINNING, there was chaos. Then came the first development model. Today, there is a multitude of different models, which all have their strengths and weaknesses. For our part, it is interesting to know how our assumptions for the test work are affected by how the rest of the project works.

4.1 The Waterfall Model

What is now called the waterfall model was described for the first time as far back as 1970 in an article by Dr. Winston Royce. The term waterfall did not exist at the time, but came into use at a later date. We must remember that, at the time the article was written, there were completely different assumptions applying to the development of software. The commonest way of developing new programs, according to Royce, was to analyse the situation and then write code until it worked. This worked for small, free-standing programs but not for more complex ones.[14]

In the article, there are several different graphs which describe suggestions for the development process. Royce says, right from the start, that the first simple model has both risks and problems. Therefore, he advocates a model with iterative inputs and also proposes the following five measures for improvement:

1. Overarching program design should take place before the analysis starts.
2. The first rule of managing software development is the ruthless application of documentation requirements.
3. Conduct a pilot version of the project from start to finish.
4. Plan, check and supervise testing. Most defects are simple ones and can be detected by visual examination. Test all routes through the code.
5. Involve the client.

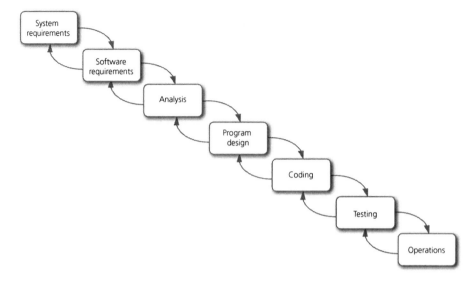

Figure 4.1: Picture No 3 in Royce's article. The original development model with certain iterative features. One of several different pictures presented.

If you study the model as it is used today, it is clear that many who professed to follow Royce's original article stopped reading after the first few pages. Modern interpretations are completely lacking in the critical points of view Royce dealt with. Besides this, he never called it the waterfall model.

The basic idea behind the linear method of attack is that it costs more to correct the design and the requirements, the further we are into the project. Therefore, it pays to have a well thought-out design, and clear goal profile, before we start writing code. Satisfactory documentation means that we do not become quite as person dependent, and that all participants in the project have the same view of what matters. Many people also like the structure and relatively simple way of working which is presented. Larger organisations like NASA, the US Department of Defense and the US Air Force have their own waterfall models.

The argument against the model is that it only works in theory. We can never finish one step completely before going to the next one. It is also impossible to know all the requirements from the start. Its weakness is also that immensely heavy emphasis is placed on documentation, which means that changes during the course of the project are very long-winded to carry out.[15] Despite these limitations, most of the more modern development models in existence are built on the fact that the process is divided up into several different steps and the work is carried out in smaller segments, precisely as Royce advocated in 1970.

4.1.1 The Effect on Testing

An elementary problem in testing is the fact that we are coming into the project at an extremely late stage and, therefore, cannot be on hand early to assure quality. The risk is that we end up with a test of the *big-bang* type – everything in one go. One benefit of sound documentation is that we possess an excellent basis to work from, since both requirements and design are properly examined by other participants in the project.

4.2 The V-model

When testing started to increase in importance there came the next version development model. The V-model, which is widely known in the world of testing, is also hotly debated. It will certainly survive for many more years and, used the right way, I regard it as extremely useful. Like all models, it is a simplification of reality and not a precise description of how the work actually proceeds. I see it as a conceptual model, which shows the relationship between test basis, i.e., the information that the tests are based on, and tests, and how the test work begins with the review of the test basis on the left-hand side, while execution of the tests is described on the right side. It can even be divided into three layers, where the lowest layer is connected to the developer and their component tests, the central one to us testers in the project team, and our system tests, and the highest to the customer or end-user, who uses the acceptance test as a way of approving the delivery of what they have ordered.

A common mistake is to draw up a time-scale from left to right, and then to try following it. This I regard as an oversimplified and, nearly always, completely invalid model of the complicated work involved in working in a project team. Remember that it is a model and, as such, it is a massive simplification of reality.

As a tester, you regularly have to adapt to the method that your project team chooses to work with. A really good tester analyses every new situation and makes the best of it. A good tester is one who delivers advantage through his or her work, and as such, you often become greatly valued by the other participants in the project.

I have seen several different variants of the V-model and do not know which one should be counted as the «right one». As long as you do not try to put more into the model than you have to go on, the version below works well.

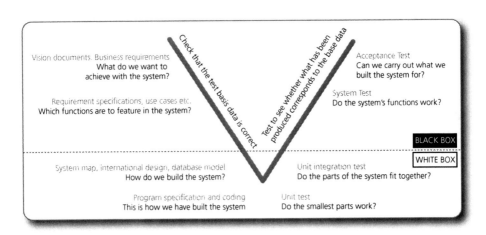

Figure 4.2: A simple variant of the V-model. The central fact is that we identify different test levels, and also that the work is divided up into preparation and execution. Setting a time-scale running from left to right does not work especially well.

For practical reasons, you divide the test work into a number of test levels from the component test to the acceptance test. The term 'test phases' is also common but, under the ISTQB standard, it is called a level or stage, and phase is the term for an activity which lasts for a specific amount of time. How many levels there are, and how much each level comprises, depends on what scope the project has. Every level has a different test basis for the test cases, even if certain test basis are used for several levels. In the diagram, we can see the connections between test levels, tasks and what test basis are present. Note that the test basis can be used as input for several different levels.

If the system being tested has many external system connections, you can add an extra level between the system test and the acceptance test, which is called a system integration test. How exact the subdivision is depends upon the formality of the test. I have been involved in variants of this, from all five levels to a single level, where we threw together a program integration test, a system test and an acceptance test, into a single level which we called a system test.

The left-hand part of the V shows the different test basis compiled in the form of requirements and design. There are a great many different variants of what they are called, so there is no general designation which is always correct. As a test designer, it is important to be involved at an early stage in order to verify all the test basis – especially the requirements. Your task is to check the quality of the material against which you are to test the completed system. Your review and analysis is important as quality assurance for the test basis. It is done best when the operational staff are involved in the testing from an early stage.

The right-hand part of the V involves checking what is in place through executing test cases, from the test basis found on the left-hand side. How involved you are, as a test designer, in the early test levels depends on how your project team works. Since these levels are extremely technical and require the close participation of the developers, for practical reasons it is not uncommon for you, as the tester, to first enter the scene at system test. However, I have my own experience of actively taking part as a tester in the component tests with good results.

4.2.1 The Effect on Testing

The V-model is good since it places its focus on testing and, additionally, structures the work into several different layers. A common mistake is to try to put more information into it than belongs there. The risk is that the connection between test levels and test basis are interpreted as though only one form of test basis are used per test level, which is usually not the case. Mischievous voices may say that it is only another way of drawing the waterfall model, but they completely miss the point of the different test levels which the V-model provides, and which are wholly absent in the waterfall model.

4.3 The W-model

An even more test-centred variant of development model is the *W-model*, which was introduced by Paul Herzlich in 1993.[16] A similar model is *the Dotted U-model* by Ed Kit[17]. Both these models emphasise that, for every activity in the chain of development, there is a corresponding test activity. The aim of the W-model is to fix the V-model's greatest flaws.

The first flaw of the V-model is that there is seldom a perfect one-to-one relationship between the development ladder and its documentation on the left-hand side, and the test activities on the right-hand side. Taking the system test as an example, both test basis, in the form of functional requirements, and also business requirements and certain parts of the technical design are used. The second flaw is that it includes nothing about static testing. The emphasis is on the execution of tests on the right-hand side of the V, but nothing is said about the review of the test basis. This is a serious flaw that we must address.

In contrast to how the V-model operates, with its focus on different test levels, the W-model focuses on the actual development products that are compiled. Every development activity has a corresponding test activity. The aim of the test activities is to determine whether the delivered product fulfils its requirements.

The important thing is that the W-model focuses specifically on the product risks at the point in time where testing can be at its most effective. Sometimes this is review, sometimes dynamic testing.

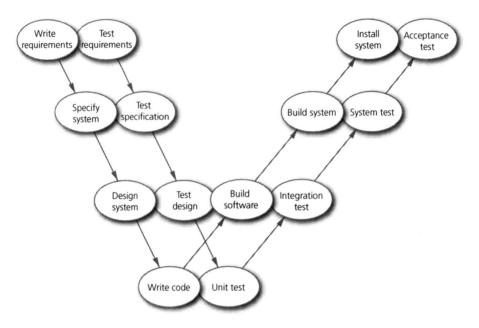

Figure 4.3: The original W-model for testing. Every development activity has a corresponding test activity. The W model focuses specifically on the product risks at the point in time where testing can be at its most effective. Sometimes this is review, sometimes dynamic testing.

4.3.1 The Effect on Testing

Greater focus on addressing actual risks through active working with the test basis, when it becomes available. The W-model is more flexible than the V model, and removes the artificial requirement to have the same number of dynamic test levels as there are development levels. Regardless of whether the compilation of requirements, the design and the coding are done in three or five steps, we can still have three test levels if it suits us. There is no requirement for certain documents that are compiled to be used for a particular test level, although this is often the case. This flexibility means that the model suits newer development models like Unified Process better. You adapt the model, according to how many steps in the design and how many test levels you want.

ESSENTIAL SOFTWARE TEST DESIGN

4.4   Unified Process

The Unified Process, UP[18], is a way of working which has enjoyed a huge breakthrough in recent years. The variant we usually come into contact with is called the Rational Unified Process, the original version, originally proposed by Jacobsen, Rumbaugh and Booch. The details may differ, but the basics are the same. The UP is built around six practices which are meant to address problems you have with the development of software. They are as follows: [19]

1. Develop iteratively – small sections, on a risk-driven basis
2. Handle requirements – use cases, requirement analysis
3. Use component-based architecture – on an object-orientated basis
4. Model software visually – graphical models
5. Verify software quality continuously – early testing
6. Handle changes to the software – control over changes

4.4.1   Phases in the Process

Projects using the UP are divided into phases which focus on different things, each phase containing one or more iterations. Every iteration delivers something which is totally complete and, in most cases, they are rounded off by testing: more about this in the next section. The basic idea is that the whole process focuses on risks, but there are different types of risk that are handled in the different phases. *Inception* starts by understanding the vision lying behind the reason why this new system is needed. The project team should be established and the participants should understand the problem. *Elaboration* builds the foundations of the system and focuses on architecture. In this phase, the most important risks relating to the architecture are handled. *Construction* is the phase where the system is developed. The most important point for decision making is between *Elaboration* and *Construction*. Here, the focus is on building functionality, and on achieving a good level of quality. In *Transition*, no new functionality is developed but, here the focus is on the end user, in order to deliver and attain the final quality.

4.4.2   The Effect on Testing

The test work follows on, and takes on different forms depending on the phase in progress. Inception, in the majority of cases, includes no execution of any test cases. Testing on architecture during Elaboration has the aim of proving that the architecture holds together. Some functionality is tested, but this is about proving that it works, not of attaining perfect quality. Construction has more of the classic type of test work about it, but divided into iterations. In

Transition, acceptance testing does occur, although the UP is extremely thin on this. All iterations in the Elaboration, Construction and Transition phases create something executable and therefore testable.

It is important to emphasise that the iterative nature of the UP has an enormous effect on testing. The UP should be configured according to need, but if it is not used iteratively, the very thing that is most useful for testing disappears. Used in the right way, this way of working means that quality consideration and management permeates every project. Early testing of small parts at a time means that we not only have the opportunity to test whether the code is right, but also objectively test the software's compliance, i.e. whether it solves our problems.[20] This approach can be compared with the W-model, which has a test activity for every development activity. Managing requirements, analysis and design are key objectives emphasised in the process, and this gives us, as testers, an excellent foundation in the form of different models from which to build test cases.

One effect which generates more work in testing, is that the number of regression tests rises when delivery of each new iteration has to be tested together with all previous parts. Automation is recommended by many people, but can be difficult if the older parts are changed and the basis for automation has to be updated a great deal, or done all over again.

4.5   Agile

There is an umbrella organisation called the *Agile Alliance* [21]which has brought together a collection of values, attitudes and principles. Under this umbrella, there are a number of system development processes which include and realise these values. *Agile* places the human in control of supporting system development without creating unnecessary work. The central point is to allow the development team to develop quickly and, at the same time, handle change by using a flexible process. The growth of *Agile* has happened as a reaction to the 'heavy' system development processes that turned out to be a hindrance, rather than of any help.

Among well known agile processes are eXtreme Programming (XP) by Kent Beck, Scrum by Ken Schwaber, Lean Software Development by Mary Poppendick, DSDM and many more. Agile's system development processes vary in character, and therefore many different processes are used successfully, which supplement each other, for example: *Scrum* and *eXtreme Programming – XP*.

All system development processes claim to address the problem with influential changes. The difference is that *Agile* welcomes change, but that does not mean that it advocates disorder and chaos. On the contrary, the methodology is often more prescriptive than in traditional system development processes, since there is a need for a strong quality and test methodology in order to be able to welcome change.

4.5.1 The Effect on Testing

The Agile development processes have enjoyed great success in promoting useful methodology in testing and quality assurance. *Extreme Programming* makes use, for example, of *test-driven development*, which involves code for component testing being written before the coding work for the program is started. [22] No code is allowed to slip through before successful component testing has been carried out. Regression testing is carried out regularly as delivery times approach thick and fast, and acceptance testing determines whether the delivery is acceptable or not. This implies that a well-executed XP project does not only deliver a system of high quality, but also code for component testing and acceptance testing material for the whole system. Thus, the management gets a stable base for continual development of the system. The testers take over code which is properly unit tested and therefore easier to continue working with.

FOOTNOTES

[13] Kit, Ed [1995]: *Software Testing in the Real World*, p.3

[14] Royce, Dr Winston [1970]: *Managing the Development of Large Software Systems*

[15] McConnell, Steve [2004]: *Code Complete* The second edition ISBN 0735619670.

[16] Herzlich, Paul [1993]: *W-model*, www.evolutif.co.uk/default.asp?page=servi ces/wmodel.html

[17] Kit, Ed [1995]: *Software Testing in the Real World*

[18] Jacobsen, Ivar, Grady Booch, Rumbaugh, James [1999]: *The Unified Software Development Process*

[19] Kruchten, Philippe [2002]: *Rational Unified Process – En introduktion* pp. 5–16

[20] *Testing for compliance with objectives is also called Validation.*

[21] *www.agilealliance.org/*

[22] Beck, Kent [2003], *Test-Driven Development*

5 APPROACHES

5.1 Test Levels

Here is a description of the distribution of tests across levels used in the standard developed by ISTQB.[23] There is no requirement for you to use all levels of testing in all projects you are working on, all the time, but, for practical reasons, it is good to have at least a couple of different levels.

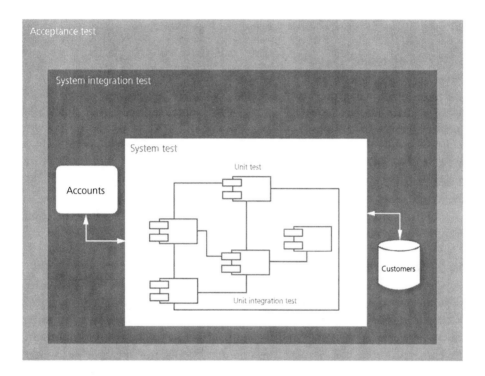

Figure 5.1: Distribution of test levels. Component testing is carried out by the developers, system testing by the development project's testers, and acceptance testing by the person who ordered the system. Every level has a different focus.

5.1.1 Unit Testing

Unit testing, also called module or component testing, is intended for checking the smallest testable parts. For this, aids are used in the form of stubs, drivers[24] or some form of tool.[25] The tests are of a technical nature and require knowledge about the programming language, so they are commonly carried out as part of the developers' coding work.

As the basis for the testers, program and design specifications are used. Test techniques suitable for this are control flow testing and data flow testing

5.1.2 Unit Integration Testing
Unit integration testing verifies interfaces between components in a system. This level is also of a technical nature, and is about piecing together components in preparation for the system tests. This level is counted amongst the structural tests and its focus is on whether the internal logic works.

5.1.3 System testing
Now, the system is tested as a whole from the users' perspective. Both functional and non-functional aspects are included. Now, we perform *behaviour-based* tests, which involve focusing on external functionality, rather than the software's inner structure.

5.1.4 System Integration Testing
If our system communicates with other systems, it can be a good idea to divide the system tests into two, by adding an extra level. This is, firstly, to check whether the system works in its own right, and then to check all the external connections in place.

5.1.5 Acceptance Testing
Acceptance testing is a means for customers to approve what has been delivered. In simple terms, it can be said that if the system does not solve the problems it was built to solve, we have not been successful. This level is often part of closing a deal between the customer and the supplier and, as such, is very important. Acceptance testing can also be a way for a production organisation to get approval for production.

To emphasise the importance of acceptance testing, here are two examples.
Example 1: Company A orders a system for ticket booking and administration. The assignment is carried out by a consultancy at a fixed price. The price means that the supplier does the least possible amount of work for the sum they have been paid. As soon as the customer has approved what has been delivered, they stop developing the system any further. All changes after approval go on a separate account. In this case, the acceptance tests were non-existent and Company A does not, therefore, discover that the system has severe quality

problems at the point of delivery. These had to be corrected afterwards, and the final bill was double the original estimate. Had Company A carried out a proper acceptance tests, the consultancy firm would have been obliged to carry out all the required corrections in order that the system fulfilled the original requirement specification as part of the original fixed price contract.

Example 2: Company B orders a new administrative system for handling insurance policies, again at a fixed price. The consultancy taking on the assignment quotes a price lower than its competitors and therefore wins the competition stage. Since the estimate is so much lower than the others, Company B actually decides to check that they are getting what they ordered. They deploy a practised test manager, who sets up a thorough acceptance test with support from a group of operations experts. Over the first three deliveries, the acceptance tests show that the system does not succeed in meeting the requirements in the contract, and is therefore returned to the supplier. Only after lengthy delays does the supplier get approval on its system. The work put in on the acceptance test by Company B saved several millions on the final bill.

5.1.6 Test Levels in Production

The last verification before you go to production with a system is to check whether the system works:

- with the volumes of data which will be present
- in the environment in which it is intended to be used
- with any connections to other elements
- together with other systems being run in the same environment

Use a test environment that is as close to its production setting as possible, and preferably the final environment. If possible, you should use the production data under controlled conditions, otherwise try to generate fake data of the same size as the system has to be able to deal with. If you are going to sell the application on the open market, you should include details about what performance requirements it satisfies, and in which environments it works. All the documentation about installation and ownership should be included.

If you use production data in any phase, remember that this type of test places heavy requirements on security and integrity, and must be carried out under controlled conditions, together with the production staff and, perhaps even specialists in load testing. It is generally illegal to use genuine data in test situations, but several companies end up unwittingly in the spotlight each year because they have not only used data in an unauthorised manner, but have also managed to send the test results out to real customers. For legal reasons, I will refrain from giving any actual examples of this.

Sometimes, you run something called a pilot for a limited number of end users. This is a way of being able to work with real production environments and real data, and of having actual end users carry out the work.

Areas where you often detect defects are:
- response times to end users are too long
- batch processes done daily, monthly or yearly take too much time
- memory or database capacity is insufficient
- parameters for connections outside the system differ between testing and production
- the data communication network cannot cope with the load
- the system is attacked by, or itself attacks, other systems

For those parts relating to load, a tool is often required. In such cases, you often bring in specialists in the field who carry out these tests according to specifications that the test group have compiled. Remember that the person who is to carry out the test has to know which type of user groups there are, how many in each group may work simultaneously and what functions they will be using. This is called compiling user profiles, also known as operational profiles. Not least do they have to know what they are to measure, and preferably, what the response time requirements are! Otherwise, it becomes more a case of stating that under these conditions we have these response times, and will that do?

There are a number of other activities which are called tests by some people. One of them is where an application is run on a *pilot basis*. This means that we work, as in real time, but with a limited number of users who know that they are the first to use the system. The object is to verify actual use in the production environment.

Another variation is what is called beta-testing. If we sell a product commercially, we can choose to distribute an early version in order to obtain end users' views and to have time to deal with potential defects and technical glitches, which only show up during actual use by real users on their site.

5.2   Which Tests Do We Run?

One suggestion for an approach is to start from what a test is worth in relation to its cost, where this value is directly related to the risk. This means that a test case of relatively little benefit to us is only worth running if it is cheap enough.[26]

The same principle is used when we have to decide which requirements are to be included in a release/iteration of a project. This applies regardless of the approach we have chosen to develop the system. This way of thinking is an alternative to a wholly risk-based approach.

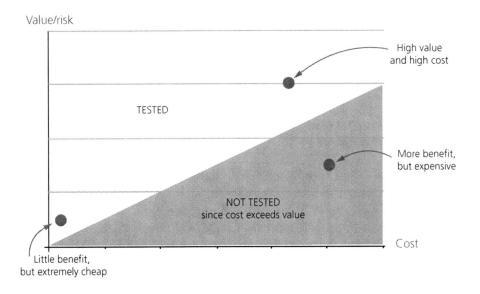

Figure 5.2: Cost is compared to value when we are choosing which tests to carry out. Tests of limited value can be carried out if their cost is very low.

5.3 Scripted Testing

The traditional approach, that stems both from the waterfall model and the V-model, means that a project is linear, and that one activity is completed in full before the next one starts. This means that all requirements are clearly stated before coding begins, and that the testers only begin when the coding is complete. This also means that all test cases must be fully specified, with the expected results, before test execution begins. This traditional method is often called *scripted testing* to distinguish it from *exploratory testing*. The obvious problems with scripted testing, when applied in reality, have led to great debate in the testing world, between those who consider that all test cases, and their expected results, can and must be documented in full before the tests are run, and those who say that we can never know everything we need to know in advance. Out of this was born the concept of exploratory testing, which involves test design work carrying on in parallel with the test execution. This is described in full in the next chapter.

A number of reasons why you write down all the information in advance are:
1. Legal or regulatory requirements, for example, in the aerospace industry, medical or other safety-critical work
2. Complex relationships which mean that you must prepare test data in detail
3. The person who has to carry out the test case must have the information in detail
4. You make the judgement that it is most effective to write down a great deal in advance
5. You know enough about how the finished system will look to be able to design effective test cases up front
6. You need the test cases for the archive or for regression testing

All operations which handle «life and death» services and products have safety as their most important governing requirement for product and service development. This applies to sectors such as aircraft, the space industry and pharmaceuticals. In the pharmaceutical field, the threat of an inspection by the US Federal Drug Administration is a great one. The risk of having your sales licence withdrawn in the largest market there is (the USA) means that all quality management work has to be documented in order to show what you have done. Many people I have spoken to say that the enormous amount of administrative and documentation work means that an extremely large part of their resources are focused in this area, and so the tests, in reality, are less effective than under a less formal approach. Obviously, well documented tests can also be supplemented with exploratory tests in order to minimise the risks further, which also happens.

5.4   The Context-Driven School
An interesting viewpoint on testing is summarised by something called *The Context-Driven School*.[27] The basic idea is that the testing depends on the context, and there are great similarities with *Agile* development. There are seven fundamental rules:
1. The value of each practice depends on its context.
2. There is good practice in its own context, but there is no best practice which applies at all times.
3. People who work together are the most important part of how every project fits together.

4. The project is developed over time in a way which often cannot be predicted.
5. The product is a solution: if the problem is not solved, the product does not work.
6. Good software testing is a challenging intellectual process.
7. Simply through judgement and skill, put into practice together throughout the whole project, we can do the right thing at the right time in order to test our products effectively.

Consequences of the above:

It pays to produce different results within a test to the extent that they satisfy the relevant requirements of the interested parties. That means that neither documentation nor anything else is compiled for its own sake, if it does not add value.

Different types of test detect different types of defect. If a program appears to be stable under one set of test techniques, it is time to change techniques.

Rather than seeing automation as a way of cutting costs, by means of a machine doing imperfectly what a human does, see it as a way of carrying out tasks which would be difficult to achieve manually.

Supporters of this school make regular use of exploratory testing.

5.5   Striking the Golden Balance

There may be laws and directives requiring formal documentation, as in the medical industry. There may be practical requirements for detailed planning, such as an extremely large number of interfaces and mutually-connected data dispersed over several systems. In such cases, we plan and document carefully in advance.

Other situations mean that we are not delivered what we expected, and changed or new functionality may have crept in. Situations can arise that we really have not prepared ourselves for, so we use exploratory testing. Since defects rarely come alone, there are often several others close to where you found the first one. The work you do in isolating the defect, and finding out whether there are defects close by, is not written into the test case: you must improvise. This can be seen as an example of exploratory testing.

I have had discussions with many experienced testers of critical systems in medical science, who carry out a whole range of carefully documented tests because of legal requirements, They supplement this work with exploratory tests with good results. However well they design the prepared test cases, there are still defects which are first detected in the more free-form part of the testing.

Earlier, we concluded that variation is good, both for test design, and for the question of which people participate. This seems to also apply to the test approach, where we successfully combine thoroughly prepared test cases with a more exploratory approach. So, in reality, we do carry out both scripted and exploratory testing in every project. We find ourselves somewhere on the scale in the diagram below.[28]

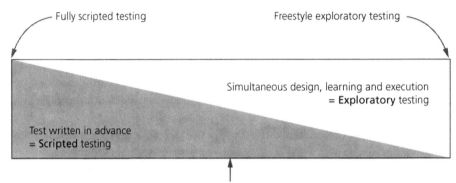

Figure 5.3: Most often, the tests consist of a mixture of scripted and exploratory testing. Some parts are scripted and others are supplemented afterwards.

FOOTNOTES

[23] *ISTQB course plan version 0.2. www.sstb.se*

[24] *Code used to execute other code*

[25] *For example, the XUnit tools, J-Unit for Java, N-Unit for C# and .Net*

[26] Bach, James [2005]: *Rapid Testing course material.*

[27] www.context-*driven-testing.com*

[28] Bach, James [2005]: *Rapid Testing course material.*

6 EXPLORATORY TESTING EXPLAINED

THIS CHAPTER IS written by James Bach and is published with the consent af the author.

> *Exploratory software testing is a powerful approach, yet widely misunderstood. In my experience, it can be orders of magnitude more productive than scripted testing. All testers who create tests at all practice some form of exploratory testing, yet many don't even realize it. Few of us study this approach, and it doesn't get much respect in our field. This attitude is beginning to change as companies seek ever more agile and cost effective methods of developing software.*

It's hard to explain something to people who think they already know it. We all know how to listen, how to read, how to think, and how to tell anecdotes about the events in our lives. As adults, we do these things everyday. Yet the *level* of any of these skills, possessed by the average person, may not be adequate for certain special situations. Psychotherapists must be *expert* listeners and lawyers *expert* readers; research scientists must *scour their thinking* for errors and journalists report stories that transcend parlor anecdote.

So it is with exploratory testing (ET): simultaneous learning, test design and test execution. This is a simple concept. But the fact that it can be described in a sentence can make it seem like something not worth describing. Its highly situational structure can make it seem, to the casual observer, that it has no structure at all. That's why textbooks on software testing, with few exceptions, either don't discuss exploratory testing, or discuss it as a straw man to be hacked to bits as an unworthy practice.

6.1   Exploratory Testing Defined

I've tried various definitions of exploratory testing. The one that has emerged as the all-around favorite among my colleagues is this:

> *Exploratory testing is simultaneous learning, test design, and test execution.*

In other words, exploratory testing is any testing to the extent that the tester actively controls the design of the tests as those tests are performed and uses information gained while testing to design new and better tests.

Defining exploratory testing (let's call it ET) is easy, just as you might say that juggling is easy to define. Doing it well is more difficult.

Have you ever solved a jigsaw puzzle? If so, you have practiced a simple form of exploratory testing. Consider what happens in the process. You pick up a piece and scan the jumble of unconnected pieces for one that goes with it. Each glance at a new piece is a test case («Does this piece connect to that piece? No? How about if I turn it around? Well, it almost fits but now the picture doesn't match...»). Instead of looking for problems, you're looking for connections, but otherwise it's the same sort of thinking. It is pretty straightforward to test if two pieces fit together, but the choice and progression of which pieces to pick up in the first place is not so simple. There is no sure way to know when you start the puzzle which «tests» to run and in what order.

But it isn't a random selection, either. This is where skill comes in. You home in on shape, color, or pattern. You might sort the pieces into little piles, first. You might flip them all face up. If you find you've got a big enough block of pieces assembled, you might move it into the frame of the puzzle to find where it connects with everything else. You may feel disorganized from time to time, and when that happens, you can step back, analyze the situation, and adopt a more specific plan. If you work on one kind of «testing» for a while (attempting to fit border pieces together, for instance), you might switch to another kind just to keep your mind fresh. Even though you aren't handed step-by-step procedure for doing it, solving a jigsaw puzzle well is a systematic process—just as is the design of software tests.

Notice how the process *flows*, and how it remains continuously, *each moment*, under the control of the practitioner. Notice that the ideas guiding it do not come from someone telling you what to do. You follow no written instructions. New ideas and strategies occur to you as the pattern of the puzzle emerges, and those ideas originate with you. Each puzzle piece placed is one less in the pile, making the rest of the search process a little easier. The puzzle changes as you solve it.

If you solve the same puzzle several times, your familiarity with the picture and the pieces will allow you to do the job more quickly. You will have a better idea of how to sort the pieces, it's even possible that you may script the process by putting an ID code on the back of each piece (there is at least one jigsaw puzzle I've seen where the pieces come with numbers on the back). But the first time through, you learn as you go. You can't avoid the learning if you want to solve the puzzle.

If you happened to know in advance exactly where each piece is supposed to go, then it would no longer be a jigsaw *puzzle*— it would be a jigsaw assembly process. You could then have a method to put it together much more efficiently, but then it would not longer resemble a testing process. In testing, I don't know where the bugs are going to be when I start. I'm not even sure where the risks are, most of the time. When I test, I puzzle over the problem of what the next test should be. The specifics of that puzzle, as they emerge through the process of solving that puzzle, affect my choice of tests as I go. This feedback dynamic— think a little, test a little, think a little more, test a little more— is at the heart of any exploratory investigation, be it for testing, development, or even scientific research or detective work.

We do many, many things in an exploratory way. Driving a car is exploratory. You don't drive by reading explicit instructions for every single movement you make. Having a conversation is exploratory. You don't go around with a prepared speech for every single occasion, do you? Much of cooking is exploratory. Most game play is exploratory. How long would you like this list to be? If you're human, then you are a creature with and exploring nature. Unleash your inner explorer and put it to work for testing.

6.2   Other Terms for Exploratory Testing

You may already know ET by another name. The phenomenon of simultaneous learning, test design and test execution is sometimes called guerilla testing, gorilla testing, monkey testing, or beta testing. I have also heard it called unstructured testing or random testing, which are terribly misleading, since it is neither unstructured nor random! A more common term for it in the literature is *ad hoc testing*. Ad hoc is a fair term. From the words «to this» in Latin, it means «formed, arranged, or done for a particular purpose only» (as opposed to being an ongoing routine). Unfortunately, ad hoc is too often connoted to mean sloppy and careless work. Just uttering «ad hoc» seems to close down the conversation.

Other popular terms pop up in organizations that believe they perform only scripted tests. In these organizations, unscripted testing activities may be embedded in other activities including bug investigation, test development, test design, or product familiarization.

In the early 1990s a group of test methodologists (now calling ourselves the Context-Driven School) began using the term «exploratory» to describe unscripted testing. With this new terminology, first published in the late 80's by Cem Kaner in his book Testing Computer Software, we sought to emphasize the dominant thought processes involved in unscripted testing, and to begin to develop the practice into a teachable discipline. Indeed, exploratory testing can be as disciplined as any other intellectual activity. Microsoft practices a formalized process of exploratory testing for the purposes of certifying third-party applications for Windows compatibility (http://www.satisfice.com/tools/procedure.pdf) and session-based test management (http://www.satisfice.com/sbtm) is a method specifically designed to make exploratory testing auditable and measurable on a wider scale.

Even though our original motivation was to avoid the baggage of the «ad hoc» label, *exploratory* is no mere euphemism. We use the word in its ordinary dictionary sense, applied to testing. Our use of the term is also consistent with the concepts of exploratory data analysis, exploratory research studies, and exploratory essays. Our usage particularly echoes its usage in geography, as the explorers of the Royal Geographic Society, in the eighteenth and nineteenth centuries, struggled with similar issues of methodology:

> «So, to qualify as exploration a journey had to be credible, had to involve hardship and risk, and had to include the novelty of discovery. Thereafter, like cricket it was somewhat hard to explain to the uninitiated. But one element was absolutely vital; indeed it was precisely that which distinguished the age of exploration from previous ages of discovery and which necessitated the adoption of the word 'exploration.' It was, quite simply, a reverence for science.»
>
> - JOHN KEAY, THE PERMANENT BOOK OF EXPLORATION

6.3   Think of it as an Approach, Not a Technique

What we call test techniques are specific heuristics for designing and performing tests. ET is not a test technique, but rather an approach. This is an important practical distinction, because ET does not stand alone or apart from test techniques. Any test technique I know can be approached in an exploratory way. Putting it on a list of techniques would be confusing, as if all the other techniques on the list, such as *boundary testing* or *equivalence class partitioning*, could not be performed in an exploratory way.

Another approach to testing is *scripting*. Scripted testing is the opposite of exploratory testing.

6.4   Exploratory vs. Scripted Testing

When I say «scripted test» I mean a set of instructions for executing a test. In pure scripted testing, tests are specified in advance of test execution. Tests are not changed while execution is underway, nor are they routinely changed based on any learning that might happen while performing the test.

It can be tricky to talk about scripted testing, especially when comparing it to exploratory testing, because the term scripted testing is often used to refer to scripted test *execution* (ignoring test design). But when comparing ET to ST, you have to include the entire process of learning about the product and constructing and debugging the test procedures. The test design process must happen, one way or another, or there will be no test procedures.

Although scripted testing is the opposite of exploratory testing, the two approaches are not mutually exclusive. It's more helpful to see them as opposite ends of the on continuum. Most real life tests are some blend of exploratory and scripted behavior.

The scripted approach to testing and the exploratory approach can actually enhance each other. The same test might exploratory in some ways and scripted in other ways. A fully scripted test informs the tester what to do and what to look for. But if a test tells you exactly what input to give the software, without telling you how you will know that a bug has occurred, then the test must rely on you to supply that part of the test design. You will have to improvise it. Many test scripts I review that are intended to be performed by hand are not specified in great detail. Some tests are specified in just few words, such as «try long inputs», which require substantial judgment and background knowledge to perform them as actual tests.

Because of the scripted/exploratory continuum, the question «Are you doing exploratory testing?» might be better stated as «In what ways and to what degree is your testing exploratory or scripted?» The skilled tester knows how to ask and answer this question.

6.5 How to Identify Exploratory Testing

If learning, test design, and test execution overlap, then that testing is exploratory to the degree that they overlap. Perfect overlap means pure, freestyle exploratory testing. In practice, a good way to spot ET in a test execution process is to ask where the test design is coming from. If it is coming from someone other than the person executing the test, then that is not an exploratory process from the point of view of that tester. If the tester is controlling some parts of the test design but not others, it is a partially exploratory process.

It's important to understand what is *not* a way to identify exploratory testing: the absence of test documentation (the tester may be following someone else's oral instructions, or may be following a habit or memory of an old test that was never written down), the lack of rigor in the test design (scripted testing may be based on ideas that are vague, shallow, and ambiguous, whereas an exploratory process may be driven by the highest conceivable rigor), or lack of repeatability (just because someone tells you to do something doesn't mean you can or will repeat it if they tell you again). Lack of documents, rigor and repeatability may characterize scripted testing as well as exploratory testing.

By definition, it is only the relationship between the thought processes of learning, test design, and test execution that characterizes exploratory testing. Because it is a continuum, when I use the term exploratory testing and don't qualify it, I mean testing that is closer to pure ET than it is to pure scripted testing. When I want to talk about testing that is pure or very close to pure exploratory testing, with no script or outside direction whatsoever, I call it *freestyle* exploratory testing.

6.6 Why Talk About ET?

I often say that *all* testers perform exploratory testing in one way or another. This causes some to wonder why I advocate this approach. What does it mean to advocate a way of testing that everybody already does? Do I also lecture my clients and students on the importance of breathing and eating?

The truth is I do not «advocate» exploratory testing. I advocate learning how to do ET well. Everybody does it, yes, but most do it poorly! Few can explain or defend that quality of their work. Few can teach exploratory techniques. This is not a difficult problem to solve, but it's one our industry has ignored for too long. Instead there is a popular fantasy that all testing should be expressed in canned thoughts that are laid down on paper. Scripting is a helpful approach, when used in moderation. It is typically not used in moderation. It has become a dangerous obsession in the software industry.

Our industry is strangely reticent to accept that testing is a product of our minds, and that it is possible to train our minds to test better and to talk articulately about how our minds work. I think it is not only possible, it's mandatory. Excellent intellectual work requires that we look at the details of our thought processes. We cannot systematically achieve excellence in testing unless we do so.

To get good at ET, we first must admit that it exists and learn how to see it. But why should we get good at ET at all? *Because it is a fabulously productive approach to testing.* Try it, compare it carefully to scripted testing, and I'm confident you'll agree.

6.7 Exploratory Testing From the Outside

The external structure of ET is easy enough to describe. Over a period of *time*, a *tester* interacts with a *product* to fulfill a testing *mission*, then *reporting* results. There you have the basic external elements of ET: time, tester, product, mission, and reporting. The mission is fulfilled through a continuous cycle of aligning ourselves to the mission, conceiving questions about the product that if answered would also allow us to satisfy our mission, designing tests to answer those questions, and executing tests to get the answers. Often our tests don't fully answer the questions, so we adjust the tests and keep trying (in other words, we explore). We must be ready to report our status and results at any time.

An exploratory test session often begins with a charter, which states the mission and perhaps some of the tactics to be used. The charter may be chosen by the tester himself, or assigned by the test lead or test manager. Sometimes charters are written down. In some organizations, test cases and procedures are documented so vaguely that they essentially serve as charters for exploratory testing.

Here are some example testing charters for DecideRight, a decision analysis product:

- Explore and analyze the product elements of DecideRight. Produce a test coverage outline.
- Identify and test all claims in the DecideRight manual. (either use checkmark/ X/? notation on the printed manual, or list each tested claim in your notes)
- Define work flows through DecideRight and try each one. The flows should represent realistic scenarios of use, and they should collectively encompass each primary function of the product.
- We need to understand the performance and reliability characteristics of DecideRight as decision complexity increased. Start with a nominal scenario and scale it up in terms of number of options and factors until the application appears to hang, crash, or gracefully prevent user from enlarging any further.
- Test all fields that allow data entry (you know the drill: function, stress, and limits, please)
- Analyze the file format of a DecideRight scenario and determine the behavior of the application when its elements are programmatically manipulated. Test for error handling and performance when coping with pathological scenario files.
- Check UI against Windows interface standards.
- Is there any way to corrupt a scenario file? How would we know it's corrupted? Investigate the feasibility of writing an automatic file checker. Find out if the developers have already done so.

- Test integration with external applications, especially Microsoft Word.
- Determine the decision analysis algorithm by experimentation and reproduce it in Excel. Then, use that spreadsheet to test DecideRight with complex decision scenarios.
- Run DecideRight under AppVerifier and report any errors.

If you find any of these charters ambiguous, I'm not surprised. They are intended to communicate the mission of a test session clearly and succinctly to testers who have already been trained in the expectations, vocabulary, techniques and tools used by the organization. Remember, in ET we make maximum use of skill, rather than attempting to represent every action in written form.

In freestyle exploratory testing, the only official result that comes from a session of ET is a set of bug reports. In session-based test management, each session of ET also results in a set of written notes that are reviewed by the test lead. It may also result in updated test materials or new test data. If you think about it, most formal written test procedures were probably created through a process of some sort of exploratory testing.

6.8   Exploratory Testing on the Inside: A Skilled Activity

Just as a star may seem dim in the spectrum of visible light, yet burn brightly in the infrared, the simple idea of exploratory testing becomes interesting and complex when viewed in the spectrum of *skill*. Consider chess. The procedures of playing chess are far less interesting than the skills. No one talks about how wonderfully Emanuel Lasker followed the procedures of chess when he defeated Steinitz in 1894 to become world champion. The procedures of chess remain constant, it's only the choices that change, and the skill of the players who choose the next move. What makes exploratory testing interesting, and in my view profoundly important, is that when a tester has the skills to *listen*, *read*, *think* and *report*, rigorously and effectively, without the use of pre-scripted instructions, the exploratory approach to testing can be many times as productive (in terms of revealing vital information) as the scripted variety. And when properly supervised and chartered, even testers without special skills can produce useful results that would not have been anticipated by a script. If I may again draw a historical analogy, the spectacularly successful Lewis and Clark expedition is an excellent example of the role of skill in exploration:

> «Lewis was the diplomatic and commercial thinker, Clark the negotiator. Lewis, who went specially to Philadelphia for training in botany, zoology, and celestial navigation, was the

scientific specialist, Clark the engineer and geographer as well as master of frontier crafts...Both men were of great intelligence, of distinguished intelligence. The entire previous history of North American exploration contains no one who could be called their intellectual equal.»
- BERNARD DE VOTO, THE JOURNALS OF LEWIS AND CLARK

The outer trappings, inputs, and outputs of exploratory testing are worth looking at, but it is the inner structure of ET that matters most—the part that occurs inside the mind of the tester. That's where ET succeeds or fails; where the excellent explorer is distinguished from the amateur. Let's look at eight key elements that distinguish an expert exploratory tester from an amateur, and some things you can do to get better at those skills.

1. Test Design: An exploratory tester is first and foremost a test designer. Anyone can design a test accidentally. The excellent exploratory tester is able to craft tests for systematic exploration of the product. Test design is a big subject, of course, but one way to approach it is to consider it a questioning process. To design a test is to craft a question for a product that will reveal vital information.

To get better at this: Go to a feature (something reasonably complex, like the table formatting feature of your favorite word processor) and ask thirty questions about it that you can answer, in whole or part, by performing some test activity, by which I mean some test, set of tests, or task that creates tests. Identify that activity along with each question. If you can't find thirty questions that are substantially different from each other, then perform a few tests and try again. Notice how what you experience with the product gives you more questions.

Another aspect of test design is making models. Each model suggests different tests. There are lots of books on modeling (you might try a book on UML, for instance). Pick a kind of model, such as a flowchart, data flow diagram, truth table, or state diagram, and create that kind of model representing a feature you are testing. When you can make such models on napkins or whiteboards in two minutes or less, confidently and without hesitation, you will find that you also are more confident at designing tests without hesitation.

2. Careful Observation: Excellent exploratory testers are more careful observers than novices, or for that matter, experienced scripted testers. The scripted tester need only observe what the script tells him to observe. The exploratory tester must watch for *anything* unusual, mysterious, or otherwise relevant to the testing. Exploratory testers must also be careful to distinguish observation from inference, even under pressure, lest they allow preconceived assumptions to blind them to important tests or product behavior.

To get better at this: Try watching another tester test something you've already tested, and notice what they see that you didn't see first. Notice how they see things that you don't and vice versa. Ask yourself why you didn't see everything. Another thing you can do is to videotape the screen while you test, or use a product like Spector that takes screen shots every second. Periodically review the last fifteen minutes of your testing, and see if you notice anything new.

Or try this: describe a screen in writing to someone else and have them draw the screen from your description. Continue until you can draw each other's screens. Ideally, do this with multiple people, so that you aren't merely getting better at speaking to one person.

To distinguish observation from inference, make some observations about a product, write them down, and then ask yourself, for each one, did you actually see that, or are you merely inferring it? For instance, when I load a file in Microsoft Word, I might be tempted to say that I witnessed the file loading, but I didn't really. The truth is I saw certain things, such as the appearance of words on the screen that I recall being in that file, and I take those things to be evidence that the file was properly loaded. In fact, the file may not have loaded correctly at all. It might be corrupted in some way I have not yet detected.

Another way to explore observation and inference is to watch stage magic. Even better, learn to perform stage magic. Every magic trick works in part by exploiting mistakes we make when we draw inferences from observations. By being fooled by a magic trick, then learning how it works, I get insight into how I might be fooled by software.

3. Critical Thinking: Excellent exploratory testers are able to review and explain their logic, looking for errors in their own thinking. This is especially important when reporting the status of a session of exploratory tests, or investigating a defect.

To get better at this: Pick a test that you recently performed. Ask what question was at the root of that test. What was it really trying to discover? Then think of a way that you could get a test result that pointed you in one direction (e.g. program broken in a certain way) when reality is in the opposite direction (e.g. program not broken, what you're seeing is the side effect of an option setting elsewhere in the program, or a configuration problem). Is it possible for the test to appear to fail even though the product works perfectly? Is it possible for the product to be deeply broken even though the test appeared to pass? I can think of three major ways this could happen: inadequate coverage, inadequate oracle, or tester error.

Inadequate coverage means that your test doesn't touch enough of the product to fulfill its goal. (Maybe you have tested printing, but not enough different printing situations to justify confidence that the print function works.) Oracles are mechanisms or principles for recognizing a problem if it occurred. *Inadequate oracle*, then, means you used a weak method of determining whether a bug is present, and that led either to reporting something that isn't a problem or failing to notice something that is a problem. (Maybe you printed something to a file, and you verified that the file was created, but you didn't check the contents of the file.) *Tester error* means that your test design was fine, but you simply didn't notice something that happened, or used the wrong data, failed to set up the system properly for testing, etc. (Maybe you saw that the print-out looks correct, but it later turned out that you were looking at the results of a different test).

Since testing is basically an infinite process, all real-life testing involves compromises. Thus, you should be able to find many ways your tests could be fooled. The idea is to maintain awareness about the limitations of your testing. For a typical complex product, it takes lots of different tests to answer any given question with high confidence.

4. Diverse Ideas: Excellent exploratory testers produce more and better ideas than novices. They may make use of heuristics to accomplish this. Heuristics are mental devices such as guidelines, generic checklists, mnemonics, or rules of thumb. The Satisfice Heuristic Test Strategy Model (http://www.satisfice.com/tools/satisfice-tsm-4p.pdf) is an example of a set of heuristics for rapid generation of diverse ideas. James Whittaker and Alan Jorgensen's «17 attacks» is another (see *How to Break Software*).

To get better at this: Practice using the Heuristic Test Strategy Model. Try it out on a feature of some product you want to test. Go down the lists of ideas in the model, and for each one think of a way to test that feature in some way related to that idea. Novices often have a lot of trouble doing this. I think that's because the lists work mainly by pattern matching on past experience. Testers see something in the strategy model that triggers the memory of a kind of testing or a kind of bug, and then they apply that memory to the thing they are testing today. The ideas in the model overlap, but they each bring something unique, too.

Another exercise I recommend is to write down, off the top of your head, twenty different ways to test a product. You must be able to say how each idea is unique among the other ideas. Because I have memorized the heuristic test strategy model, when I am asked this question, I can list thirty-three different ways to test. I say to myself «CITESTDSFDPOCRUSPICSTMPLFSDFSCU RR» and then expand each letter. For instance, the second letter stands for information, which represents the idea «find every source of information I can about this feature and compare them to each other and to the product, looking for inconsistencies.» The «O» stands for operations, which represents the idea «discover the environment in which the product will be used, and reproduce that environment as close as I can for testing.

5. *Rich Resources:* Excellent exploratory testers build a deep inventory of tools, information sources, test data, and friends to draw upon. While testing, they remain alert for opportunities to apply those resources to the testing at hand.

To get better at this: Go to a shareware site, such as Download.Com and review the utilities section. Think about how you might use each utility as a test tool. Visit the Web sites related to each technology you are testing and look for tutorials or white papers. Make lots of friends, so you can call upon them to help you when you need a skill they have.

6. *Self-Management:* Excellent exploratory testers manage the value of their own time. They must be able to tell the difference between a dead end and a promising lead. They must be able to relate their work to their mission and choose among the many possible tasks to be done.

To get better at this: Set yourself a charter to test something for an hour. The charter could be a single sentence like «test error handling in the report generator» Set an alarm to go off every fifteen minutes. Each time the alarm goes off. Say out loud why you are doing whatever you are doing at that exact moment. Justify it. Say specifically how it relates to your charter. If it is off-charter, say why you broke away from the charter and whether that was a well-made decision.

7. *Rapid Learning:* Excellent exploratory testers climb learning curves more quickly than most. Intelligence helps, of course, but this, too, is a matter of skill and practice. It's also a matter of confidence— having faith that no matter how complex and difficult a technology looks at first, you will be able to learn what you need to know to test it.

To get better at this: Go to a bookstore. Pick a computer book at random. Flip through it in five minutes or less, then close the book and answer these questions: what does this technology do, why would anyone care, how does it work, and what's an example of it in action? If you can't answer any of those questions, then open the book again and find the answer.

8. Status Reporting: Tap an excellent exploratory tester on the shoulder at any time and ask, «What is your status?» The tester will be able to tell you what was tested, what test techniques and data were used, what mechanisms were used to detect problems if they occurred, what risks the tests were intended to explore, and how that related to the mission of testing.

To get better at this: Do a thirty minute testing drill. Pick a feature and test it. At the end of exactly thirty minutes, stop. Then without the use of notes, say out loud what you tested, how you would have recognized a problem, what problems you found, and what obstacles you faced. In other words, make a test report. As a variation, give yourself 10 minutes to write down the report.

6.9   Exploratory Testing is a Profoundly Situational Practice

Exploratory testing is testing that evolves throughout the project. How it evolves depends on what comes up. It's a puzzle we are solving, and the specifics of the testing puzzle, as they emerge through the process of solving that puzzle, affect our tactics for solving it. This truth is at the heart of any exploratory investigation, be it for testing, development, or even scientific research or detective work. What kinds of specifics affect ET? Here are some of them:

- the mission of the test project
- the mission of this particular test session
- the role of the tester
- the tester (skills, talents, and preferences)
- available tools and facilities
- available time
- available test data and materials
- available help from other people
- accountability requirements
- what the tester's clients care about
- the current testing strategy
- the status of other testing efforts on the same product
- the product, itself
  - its user interface
  - its behavior
  - its present state of execution

- its defects
- its testability
- its purpose
- what the tester knows about the product
  - what just happened in the previous test
  - known problems with it
  - past problems with it
  - strengths and weaknesses
  - risk areas and magnitude of perceived risk
  - recent changes to it
  - direct observations of it
  - rumors about it
  - the nature of its users and user behavior
  - how it's supposed to work
  - how it's put together
  - how it's similar to or different from other products
- what the tester would like to know about the product

Instead of asking what test they are instructed to run, exploratory testers ask *what's the best test I can perform, right now?* Each of the considerations, above, may influence what test is needed. These factors change continuously throughout the course of the test project, or even from moment to moment during a test session. The power of exploratory tests can be optimized throughout the test process, whereas scripts, because they don't change, tend to become less powerful over time. They fade for many reasons, but the major reason is that once you've executed a scripted test one time and not found a problem, the chance that you will find a problem on the second execution of the script is, in most circumstances, substantially lower than if you ran a new test instead.

6.10 Managing Exploratory Testing

In many organizations, it's important to distinguish between a test manager and a test lead. The test manager usually has hiring and firing authority and other administrative responsibilities, whereas the test lead is focused only on the test strategy and tactics. For the purposes of discussing ET test management, I'll use the term test lead, even though a test manager may be fulfilling that role.

Freestyle exploratory testing can be managed in two ways: delegation or participation. With delegation, the test lead specifies the charters. Then the testers go off on their own, design and execute the tests to fulfill the charters, and report back. In practice, a particular tester is often permanently assigned to one set of components, so that the project benefits from an uninterrupted learning curve. The test reports that come back may be written or oral. Cem Kaner suggests regular meetings with testers to discuss test progress, at least once per week. He finds it useful to open the meeting with a standard question, «What is the most interesting bug you've found recently? Show it to me.» In the session-based approach, test reports are written, and testers are interviewed at least once per day.

Managing by delegation essentially treats each tester as an executive who manages the value of his own time. Just as with executives, a tester who hasn't earned credibility as a productive and responsible tester is not given big assignments, but rather is restricted to shorter exploratory sessions and subjected to more scrutiny. Being a leader of exploratory testers means being a coach of semi-independent creative agents.

Managing by participation means that the leader tests right alongside the rest of the testers. In practice, this is best for leaders who have otherwise delegated their administrative and meeting attendance responsibilities to other people. Participation allows the leader to direct the test strategy in real time, and continuously demonstrate the behaviors he expects from the team. Since the test manager is ultimately responsible for the performance of the team, participation puts him in an excellent position to fulfill that responsibility. Many concerns about the potential for confusion or inefficient testing during ET tend to disappear when a test lead is intimately involved with the testing.

Most test leads will use a test coverage guide of some kind to help them organize the test effort. This guide may take the form of a test coverage outline or matrix, a list of risks, or even an old fashioned To Do list.

Team exploratory testing can be extremely powerful. In the experience of many test leads who've tried it, the social energy of people working together, hunting for bugs on the same equipment at the same time, often leads to more and better ideas than would otherwise come out if the same people worked independently. One way to organize team ET is to put testers into pairs and have them share one computer as they test. Another way I've done it is to have one tester «drive» at the keyboard while several others watch and comment. If the driving tester discovers a problem or has a question that needs to be researched, one of the watchers can break away to attempt to investigate that issue using another test platform. That frees the driving tester to continue the main thread of testing with less distraction. This method works especially useful as a blockbusting tool to get the test effort out of a rut or to help train testers in the technology of the product or about methods of test design.

6.11 Where ET Fits

The exploratory approach pervades not only software development but any intellectual pursuit. Remember that exploratory testing is on a continuum with scripted test. Most testing has at least some exploratory element to it. Look closely and you'll see for yourself.

Let's talk about *very* exploratory testing. Freestyle exploratory testing fits in any of the following situations:

- You need to provide rapid feedback on a new product or feature.
- You need to learn the product quickly.
- You have already tested using scripts, and seek to diversify the testing.
- You want to find the single most important bug in the shortest time.
- You want to check the work of another tester by doing a brief independent investigation.
- You want to investigate and isolate a particular defect.
- You want to investigate the status of a particular risk, in order to evaluate the need for scripted tests in that area.

Freestyle exploratory testing aside, ET fits anywhere that testing is not completely dictated in advance. This includes all of the above situations, plus at least these additional ones:

- Improvising on scripted tests.
- Interpreting vague test instructions.
- Product analysis and test planning.
- Improving existing tests.
- Writing new test scripts.
- Regression testing based on old bug reports.
- Testing based on reading the user manual and checking each assertion.

ET is powerful because of how the information flows backward from executing testing to re-designing them. Whenever that feedback loop is weak, or when the loop is particularly long, slow, or expensive, ET loses that power. Then, we must fall back on carefully scripted tests. Another place we might use scripted tests is in any part of our testing that will be especially controversial, or are subject to a high degree of management or customer approval. But don't settle for weak tests just because they please the auditors. Consider using a combined exploratory and scripted strategy, and get the best of both worlds.

6.12 ET in Action

To give you an example of what an exploratory tester might be thinking about as he tests, let me share one of my ET experiences.

I once had the mission of testing a popular photo editing program in four hours. My mission was to assess it against the specific standards of the Microsoft Windows Compatibility Certification Program. The procedure for performing such a test is laid out as a formalized exploratory testing process. My goal was to find any violations of the compatibility requirements, all of which were clearly documented for me.

With my charter in mind, I set myself to test. Applying one of the simplest heuristics of exploring, I chose to begin by walking through the menus of the application, trying each one. While doing so, I began creating an outline of the primary functions of the product. This would become the basis for reporting what I did and did not test, later on.

I noticed that the Save As… function led to a sophisticated set of controls that allow the user to set various attributes of image quality. Since I knew nothing about the technical aspects of image quality, I felt unprepared to test those functions. Instead, I started an issues list and made a note to ask if my client was willing to extend the time allowed for testing so that I could study documentation about image quality and form a strategy for testing it. Having made my note, I proceeded walking through menus.

A basic strategy of ET is to have a general plan of attack, then allow yourself to deviate from it for short periods of time. It's like being on a tour bus. Even though the tour bus takes you to certain places at certain times, you can still step off occasionally and wander around. The same is true with exploratory testing. There's value in seeing what you can see on the planned tour, but it's also important to occasionally look at something more closely or to investigate something that might not have been on the itinerary. Whatever you do, don't fall asleep on the tour bus— This happens to you when you adopt a plan to visit various parts of the product, then visit them without really thinking about how well the product is working. A successful exploratory tester is always questioning what happens.

My first urge to leave the tour of the menus happened when I found a dialog box in the program that allowed me to control the amount of memory used by the application. This immediately gave me an idea (sudden ideas are valued in exploratory testing). Since stability is one of the requirements of the Windows Compatibility program, I thought it would be interesting to try to destabilize the product by setting it to use the minimum amount of memory, then ask it to perform memory intensive functions. So I set the slider bar to use 5% of system memory, then visited the image properties settings and set the image size to 100 inches square. That's a big canvas. I filled the canvas with purple dots and went to the effects menu to try activating some special graphical effects.

Okay, here comes an important part: I chose a «ripple» effect from the menu and *bam*, the product immediately displayed an error message informing me that there was not enough memory for that operation. This is very interesting behavior, because it establishes a standard. I have a new expectation from this point forward: a function should be able to prevent itself from executing if there is not enough memory to perform the operation. This is a perfect example of how, in exploratory testing, the result of one test influences the next, because I then proceeded to try other effects to see if the rest of them behaved in the same way. What did I find? None of the others I tried behaved that way. Instead, they would crank away for five minutes, doing nothing I could see other than drive the hard disk into fits. Eventually an error popped up «Error -32: Sorry this Error is Fatal.» and the application crashed.

This is a nice result, but I felt that the test wouldn't be complete (exploratory testers strive to anticipate questions that their clients will ask later on) unless I set that memory usage lever all the way up, to use the most memory possible. To my surprise, instead of getting the Error -32, the entire operating system froze. Windows 2000 is not supposed to do that. This was a far more serious problem than a mere crash.

At this point in the process, I had spent about 30 minutes of a 4 hour process, and already found a problem that disqualified the application from compatibility certification. That was the good news. The bad news is that I lost my test notes when the system froze. After rebooting, I decided I had learned enough from stress testing and returned to the menu tour.

I submit that this test story is an example of disciplined, purposeful testing. I can report what I covered and what I found. I can relate the testing to the mission I was given. It was also quite repeatable, or at least as repeatable as most scripted tests, because at all times I followed a coherent idea of what I was trying to test and how I was trying to test it. The fact that those ideas occurred to me on the fly, rather than being fed to me from a document, is immaterial. I hope you see that this is a far cry from unsystematic testing.

6.13 The Productivity of ET

There are no reasonable numbers; no valid studies of testing productivity that compares ET with scripted testing. All we have are anecdotes. Here are a couple anecdotes of mine.

I have taught testing classes where exploratory testers, testing on a system that automatically logged their work, have designed and executed almost a hundred tests each. Then when challenged to write a repeatable test procedure in the same amount of time, each person managed to create only one. You can argue that the repeatable test procedure was better, in some ways, than the exploratory tests. Maybe it was or maybe it wasn't. Personally, I felt that the test scripts produced were far less powerful than were the exploratory tests.

I have led teams in the testing of applications that had already been tested by scripted means, and found dramatic problems in them. In one case, without any preparation or test materials, it took my team only ten minutes to crash a network appliance so badly that its internal hard drive had to be reformatted. True, it took longer than ten minutes to investigate and isolate the problem, but that would also have been true for a scripted test procedure, assuming it found the problem in the first place.

I helped one large company start an exploratory test team in a department surrounded by scripted testers. They found that the ET people, unencumbered by the maintenance associated with test artifacts, were able to pursue more leads and rumors about risk. They found more bugs, and more important bugs. Three years later, the team was still in place.

A man approached me at a conference and said that he ran an exploratory test team for a large telecom company. He said his team moves from project to project, and the reason he's allowed to continue his work is because their metrics show that his team find four times as many problems in a given period of time than do scripted testers.

These vignettes don't prove anything. I include them simply to pique your interest. The truth is, productivity depends upon a lot of factors. So, work with it, and gather your own experiences.

Exploratory testing can be described as a martial art of the mind. It's how you deal with a product that jumps out from the bushes and challenges you to a duel of testing. Well, you don't become a black belt by reading books. You have to work at it. Happy practicing.

6.14 Acknowledgements

This article has benefited from the hard questioning and ideas offered by the following colleagues: Cem Kaner, Lee Copeland, Brian Marick, and Dorothy Graham. Parts of this article appeared first in «Inside the Mind of the Exploratory Tester», STQE magazine, volume 5, issue 6, November/December 2003.

7 TEST DESIGN TECHNIQUES: AN OVERVIEW

7.1 Static and Dynamic Techniques

We usually differentiate between static and dynamic test design techniques. A static technique involves examining documentation, design or code, while a dynamic one involves studying the program while it is being run. Here is a diagram of a common subdivision.[29]

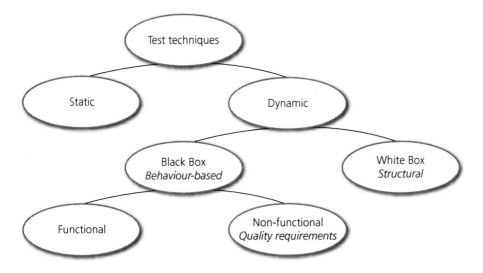

Figure 7.1: Overview of test design techniques. Dynamic techniques may focus on functions or on quality factors. Static techniques, which involve scrutinising code or documentation, are usually also counted as testing, even though no code is executed.

7.2 Static Techniques

A static test design technique involves no program code being executed. Instead different types of documentation in the form of text, models or code are analysed, often by hand. In a number of cases, e.g. in the compilation of program code, tools are used. The defects detected are often related to requirements and design: either there are parts missing or the documents are not consistent within themselves or do not conform with the standard in force. The advantages of reviews are that we intervene early and we supplement the dynamic testing by detecting other types of defects. The formality of the review is usually governed by the criticality of the material being examined. A requirements specification which is fundamental to all other work is examined more carefully than a program specification for a small part of the system. It is a question of choosing the right type of review in order to derive the greatest possible benefit. Reviews are regarded by most organisations today as valuable and are commonly used in many different sectors. I have worked with different types of reviews within telecommunications, banking, insurance and the public sector. In the majority of cases these reviews are informal, and nowhere outside the academic world have I been involved in an inspection of the kind described below.

7.2.1 Inspection

The most formal review technique is called an *inspection* and is strictly governed. The method was developed by Michael E. Fagan at IBM.[30] The participants prepare themselves carefully by examining selected areas according to role descriptions and check-lists. At the review meeting all points of view are recorded and how they are to be addressed can be discussed. On the other hand, the problems are solved afterwards. Since the way of working is formal, only a limited amount of material is examined on each occasion, mostly no more than a dozen pages, depending on the test basis. For this type of review to be effective requires the participants to be trained, check-lists to be compiled, and the review meeting itself to be chaired by an experienced moderator. For those who wish to learn more, there is a detailed description in the book *Software Inspection*[31].

7.2.2 Walkthrough

One of the simpler and less formal techniques is called walkthrough. It involves the author presenting his or her material to a selected group of participants in order to get them involved in the test basis more quickly as a result. Questions and explanations are welcomed during the meeting. The purpose is more one of creating a common picture, than of identifying defects, but the technique is still counted as static testing.

7.2.3 Technical Review

As the name suggests, a technical review focuses on the technical parts of the project like architecture and program design. Here, primarily the technical experts and the architects take part together with other developers. The purpose is both to evaluate choices of solution, and compliance with standards and other documentation. The result is often documented in a log.

7.2.4 Informal Review

Informal review involves two or more people looking through a document or code that one or the other of them has written. The purpose is still to detect defects, but there are usually no check-lists used and the result does not need to be documented.[32]

7.2.5 Modelling – an Alternative to Reviews

The method that I prefer for static testing is not listed with the techniques above. It is more a matter of analysing the test basis I have and, from it, creating models of how I believe it should work. By compiling the models and discussing them with people involved, I often detect defects in the form of information that is missing, inconsistent, or plainly wrong. We will cover modelling in detail later in the book.

7.3 Dynamic Test Design Techniques

Dynamic testing involves usmeans testing code by executing it. We usually split up the dynamic techniques into *behaviour-based*, often termed black-box, and *structural*, usually called white- or glass-box. Regardless of whether we work with behaviour-based or structural methods, there are a great many different techniques which can be used in order to create good test cases

7.3.1 Data

For handling test data, we split up the mass of values into *equivalence partitions*. For numerical intervals, most of all, there is also *boundary value* analysis for the groups we have identified. Handling test data in these ways reappears as an important part of most other techniques, and are therefore called *the elementary techniques* in this book.

7.3.2 Flows

There are flows at many different levels, from overarching business processes, to program code, which have both control flows and data flows. The principles of flow testing are similar to each other, whatever the level. Firstly, we draw up the flow graph, then we cover the variations of the flows by using branch or path analysis. This is the same principle as white box testing.

How good the test coverage needs to be, depends on risk-level and how complicated the flow is. The perhaps somewhat unsatisfactory answer is that it just depends. The lowest level of coverage that I make use of is where all branches have to be covered, and this mostly works well when it comes to more overarching flows, such as business processes. More detailed flows, such as use case flows, in the form of activity diagrams, often require you to have more combinations of different flows. There is no general rule for which level you should or must cover in order to have a good set of tests.

7.3.3 Logic: Sets of Rules, Formulae

In order to handle sets of rules and mathematical formulae, *decision tables* are powerful aids for creating test cases. In order to check whether a decision table is correct – complete and not overlapping – for some types of sets of rules, you can draw up a *decision tree*. The graph is also an excellent aid even when you run your tests and evaluate potential defects.

7.3.4 Combinatorial Analysis

A commonly occurring problem is where you have a large number of variables which can be combined with each other in an almost infinite number of variations. Testing all combinations for a range of mutually dependent variables is often not possible. We quickly get what we call a combinatorial explosion, which is common in testing.

For handling this type of problem, there are a number of useful means of simplification, without us missing too much. Elementary comparisons[33] involve all variables included in a condition being capable of determining the result of the condition at least once, and all results of the condition being obtained. Another way of combining variables is to test them with each other in pairs so that *all pairs* are covered.

7.3.5 Experience based testing

There are a great many different techniques which all build on earlier experience of what usually goes wrong. To this group belong the variants called *risk lists, error guessing, taxonomies, defect classifications and attack patterns.*

Error guessing is described in some works as a technique in its own right.[34] The purpose is to point out areas that we think have defects in them from experience, technical knowledge, old defect reports, etc. An alternative viewpoint is to see *error guessing* as a natural element of all techniques.[35] In this book, it is counted as a risk-based technique.

7.3.6 Advanced Testing

Once the individual functions in a program have been tested, it is a question of checking whether the whole works. We have already dealt with the *testing of business processes* earlier in this chapter under *Flows* ther useful techniques are the testing of *time cycles, data cycles, soap-opera testing*[36], *life cycles* and *syntax testing*. We can also work with user profiles in order to find out how the actual users will be using our application, and from this, test the relevant combinations. A technique that has worked out exceptionally well for some of my colleagues is exploratory testing using test charters which are basically a test case description without detailed steps that states the task but gives the tester great freedom to perform. The chapter on exploratory testing explains this concept further and there is an example of a simple test charter in the chapter on testing business processes.

7.4 Black, White and Grey

7.4.1 Black Box Techniques – Behaviour-Based Testing

We often call behaviour-based testing input or output data-driven testing. This is aimed at verifying whether a system behaves correctly from the outside, without us being concerned about what is happening inside – hence the commonly used expression black box testing. As a starting point, you often have a specification in the form of a use case, a work process or other requirement documentation. We ask the system a question and get an answer, and if the result corresponds to what we are expecting, the test case is completed with a satisfactory result. The fact that we are not concerned about what is happening inside the system does not necessarily mean that we do not want to know how it works. That definition, I think, is wrong. Often, from the design of the system, we can obtain valuable information which helps us generate better test cases. One example is where a developer has performed an update on a program, and we want to know which parts of the system may be affected by the change, and which regression tests we should therefore conduct. There is more about this in the section on Grey Box Testing.

7.4.2 White Box Techniques – Structural Testing

White box tests are also called structural- or glass-box tests. The purpose of the tests is to verify the internal logic in the test object. The technique is used at the component testing and program integration testing stages and requires detailed knowledge of how the system is built. The structural tests encompass *control flow* (program flow) and *data flow*. Control flow tests check that the internal program logic is working. Data flow tests verify whether the way a variable is defined, used and destroyed is handled correctly. [37]

The test basis used are program and design specifications where the details about the program's internal structure are clearly described. It is especially important to test all boundary values and error conditions carefully. You can carry out structural tests without any tools, but if you are to measure the degree of coverage this is very difficult without automated aids. Structural tests depend on programming language, and this is the help the test tools offer.

7.4.3 Combined: Grey Box Testing

Often, we make use of a combination of behaviour-based and structural techniques in order to obtain better test cases. This involves us looking into the box to determine the internal structure, in order to create better behaviour-based tests. Knowledge of programming and databases is therefore a strength when it comes to detecting more defects.[38]

7.5 Non-functional Tests

Besides pure functional requirements, there are also quality requirements. The quality factors requirements category contains so many aspects that it is appropriate to create an additional categorisation in order to make the requirements profile more visible. A good foundation for such a classification is given in the standard ISO 9126 Software Product Evaluation which describes how to structure the main non-functional requirements.

ISO 9126 [1991] states that a product's quality must be determined according to the following six headings. An appendix in the standard contains a model for how these can be interpreted, providing a number of subcategories for each heading:

1 **Functionality:** Are the desired functions present? *suitability, correctness, compatibility, compliance with standards, security*
2 **Reliability:** Is the system robust, and does it work in different situations? *maturity, error tolerance, restart (after error), accessibility*
3 **Usability:** Is the system intuitive, comprehensible and simple to use? *intelligibility, learning requirements, ownership*
4 **Efficiency:** Does the system use resources well? time aspects *(e.g. performance characteristics), resource requirements (e.g. scalability)*
5 **Maintainability:** Can the workforce, developers and users upgrade the system when needed? *analysability, modifiability, configurability, testability*
6 **Portability:** Can the system work on different platforms, with different databases, etc.? *adaptability, installation requirements, compliance with standards, replaceability*

It is important for us not to forget the above characteristics. The question is, whose responsibility is it to ensure that they work? Functionality is the part that we testers work with most, while reliability and efficiency are more technical aspects which often require some form of tool and specialist knowledge. Usability is brought into focus when the user interface is designed. This should be done by experts in usability,[39] [40] but this is too often neglected. It is not a good idea to leave this type of testing to testers who lack specialist knowledge of these issues!

ESSENTIAL SOFTWARE TEST DESIGN

7.6   How Many Design Techniques are There?

Actually, the question of how many design techniques there are is, in itself, not very interesting. What is interesting, is which techniques you need to know in order to do a good job, and how you adapt the techniques for each situation, so that they suit precisely that situation. Just because you vary a technique to suit the situation does not mean that it is a whole new technique. It is not recommended that you have a favourite technique that you always use, but rather have a range of basic techniques that you master well and can apply in different situations.

For many years, I have been learning the martial art Aikido, which is based on the self-defence techniques of the Samurai. My Sensei talks about twelve basic techniques which can be varied according to which situation you find yourself in. It is very important to master the basic techniques well, the next step being to be able to adapt your defence to your opponent and the situation. It is the precise feeling and timing which marks out a master.

Below is a selection of different organisations' views on which test techniques are important. As you will see, the way to subdivide them and what is considered important differs depending on whom you talk to.

7.7   The Selection in This Book

The techniques described in this book are the selection that I personally consider every tester should have knowledge of, and be able to apply. All these techniques are conventional and well-known in testing internationally. If you want to read more about each technique, there are plenty of references in the bibliography. In no way does this selection claim to be exhaustive, or the only one you should know about, but it is a good base to start from.

- Data: *equivalence partitions, boundary value analysis, domain testing*
- Flows: *work processes, use cases for test cases*
- Event based: *state graphs*
- Logic: *decision trees, decision tables*
- Combinational analysis: *all pairs, elementary comparisons*
- Risk-based testing: *risk, error guessing, taxonomies, heuristics, attack patterns*
- Advanced testing: *scenario-based, soap opera, time cycles, data cycles*
- For the developer: *control flow, data flow*

7.8   The ISTQB Standard

There is an international alliance called the International Software Testing Qualifications Board, ISTQB[41]. In their syllabus for accreditation on their foundation course, they deal with the test design techniques they think are the most important for functional tests. From the start, this selection builds on the British standard BS 7925:2 for component testing. In the latest official version, the following techniques are listed: [42]

1. Equivalence partitioning
2. Boundary value analysis
3. State diagrams
4. Decision tables
5. Use case testing
6. Classification tree method

They deal additionally with the following approaches:
7. Error guessing
8. Exploratory testing

For structural testing, they deal with code coverage in the form of a number of different variants where you cover all of the following:

1. Statements
2. Branches
3. Loop
4. A combination of branches and conditions (multiple combination decision coverage)

7.9   The Academic World

I asked the question of what were the most important test techniques to the well-known authority on testing, Cem Kaner, who is also a Professor at the Florida Institute of Technology, and the author of several books, and got the following answer:[43] [44]

He teaches 10 elementary techniques in his black-box testing course:

1. Function testing
2. Specification-based testing
3. Domain testing
4. Risk-based testing
5. Scenario testing
6. Regression testing
7. Stress testing
8. User testing
9. State machines
10.   Volume testing

This is what Cem says:

> «I have together with James Bach chosen these ten since they
> exemplify the most important areas within black-box testing:
>
> There is a separate course for component testing. However, the
> purpose of reading out these techniques is not to make people
> good at just ten techniques. I want the pupils to understand that
> there are a great many different variants of methodology, that they
> have fundamentally different strengths and that the skilful tester
> chooses the technique, or makes up a technique, which suits the
> needs of the day.
>
> An example of variation: some of our techniques focus on input
> and output data, others on control flows, some on interaction with
> other programs or units (this can be modelled as input/output data,
> but because the interactions often contain sequences of messages,
> it can often be better modelled as a state graph with accompanying
> data analysis). Certain techniques focus on compliance with legal
> requirements, specifications, announcements etc. Others focus on
> actual use of the product etc. All of these drive the tester towards
> new research, on a quest for different sources of information as an
> aid in design and evaluation of test cases. «

7.10 Companies Which are Far Ahead in the Field of Testing

Peter Zimmerer from Siemens in Germany presented what he calls the Test
Design Poster at EuroSTAR in December 2005[45]. The fact that I have chosen
to reproduce his whole list here is down to the fact that it is one of the most
complete catalogues I have seen. He says this:

> «The Test Design Poster contains a categorised overview of test
> design methods, paradigms, techniques, styles and ideas for how
> to generate test cases. We give it out to everyone who works in
> development and testing in order to give them inspiration. Then,
> we go out into the organisation, and show them how to use the
> different methods.
>
> Satisfactory testing requires several different methods to be used
> in combination. The choice of methods depends on many factors,
> including:

1. Requirements on the system and desired quality
2. Requirements on the tests in terms of strength and depth
3. Test strategy: which tests are performed in which parts of the chain of development
4. Existing basic test data
5. The system to be tested
6. Technique for soft- and hardware
7. Compatible tool support

The workload/difficulty of the methods, or the actual intensity of them, is divided into five layers, from 1, which is very small/simple, to 5 which is very large/difficult.

Category	Method, paradigm, technique, style and ideas for test cases	Degree of difficulty/ intensity
Black Box interfaces, data, models	Standards, norms, formal specifications, requirements	3
	Criteria, functions, interfaces	1
	Requirement - based with traceability matrix	3
	Use case based (activity diagram, sequence diagram)	3
	CRUD, Create, Read, Update, Delete (database operations)	3
	Scenario tests, soap opera tests	4
	User profiles: frequency and priority/critical(reliability)	4
	Statistical testing (Markov chains)	4
	Random (ape testing)	4
	Design with contract (built - in self test)	3
	Equivalence Groups	2
	Classification trees	3
	Domain tests, category partition	4
	Boundary value analysis	2
	Special values	1
	Test catalogue for input data values, input data fields	5
	State Graphs	3
	Cause - effect graphs	5
	Decision tables	5
	Syntax tests (grammar)	4
	Combinatory testing (pair tests)	3
	Evolution tests	5
Grey - box	Dependences/relationships between classes, objects, methods, functions	2
	Dependences/relationships between components, services, applications, systems	3
	Communication behaviour (dependence analysis)	3
	Tracking (passive testing)	3
	Protocol based (sequence diagram)	4

Figure 71a Test Design Poster part 1

White - box	Control flows	Coverage	Statements	2
Internal structure, paths		(code - based, model - based)	Branches	3
			Conditions	4
			Interfaces	4
		Static measurement	Cyclomatic complexity (McCabe)	4
			Measurement (e.g, Halstead)	4
	Data flows		Read/write	3
			Define/use	5
Positive, valid cases	Normal, expected construction			1
Negative, invalid cases	Unauthorised construction			3
	Defect management			3
	Exception management			5
Defect - based	Risk - based			2
	Systematic defect analysis (FMEA: Failure Mode and Effect Analysis)			4
	Defect catalogues, bug taxonomies (Biezer, Kaner)			4
	Attack patterns (Whittaker)			3
	Defect models which depend on the technology and nature of the system			2
	Defect patterns: standard patterns or from root cause analysis			3
	Defect reports (previous)			2
	Error guessing			2
	Test patterns (Binder), Question patterns (Q - patterns: Vipul Kochar)			3
	Ad Hoc, intuitive, based on experience			1
	Exploratory testing, heuristics			2
	Mutation tests			5
Regression testing	Parts which have changed			1
	Parts affected by the changes			2
	Risky, highly prioritised, critical parts			3
	Parts which are often changed			3
	Everything			5

Figure 71b Test Design Poster part 2

ESSENTIAL SOFTWARE TEST DESIGN

7.11 Other Sources

There are many further sources where you can find lists of techniques. Some of the best known are the recent new version TMAP Next [46], which is widespread in countries like the Netherlands and Belgium. Boris Beizer has written a couple of classic works on testing techniques: Software Testing Techniques[47] and Black Box Testing Techniques[48]. Finally, there is Glenford Myers' book The Art of Software Testing[49] from 1979, which was one of the first to be written in the field. Many of his ideas stand up well even today and there is hardly a single new book on testing on the market which does not contain a reference to this book.

FOOTNOTES

[29] ISTQB [2005]: *Course plan*, chapter 4

[30] Fagan, Michael[1976]: *Design and Code inspections to Reduce Errors in Program Development.* IBMSystems Journal, 15(3), pp. 182–211

[31] Gilb, Tom, Graham, Dorothy [1993]: *Software Inspection*

[32] Weinberg, Gerald[1971]: *The Psychology of Computer Programming*

[33] Pol, Martin, Teunissen, Ruud, van Veenendaal, Erik [2002] *Software Testing – A Guide to the TMAP Approach* pp. 219–223

[34] Myers, Glenford [1979] *The Art of Software Testing*, p.37

[35] Beizer, Boris [1995], *Black Box Testing* p. xiv

[36] *Soap-opera testing, in short, is about thinking through all the strange and extreme cases that can arise.*

[37] Copeland, Lee [2003]: *A Practitioner´s Guide to Software Test Design* pp. 139–142

[38] Copeland, Lee [2003]: *A Practitioner´s Guide to Software Test Design* p. 8, and Whittaker, James [2003]: *How to Break Software* pp. 57–58

[39] *www.funkanu.se*

[40] Cooper, Alan[2004]: *The Inmates are Running the Asylum*

[41] *www.istqb.org*

[42] *ISTQB course plan version 0.2.*

[43] Kaner, Cem [2005] *groups.yahoo.com/group/software-testing/message/2880*

[44] *www.testingeducation.org/BBST/BBST--IntroductiontoTestDesign.html*

[45] Zimmerer, Peter [2005]: *Eurostar presentation*

[46] Koomen et al [2006] *TMAP Next*

[47] Beizer, Boris, [1993] *Software Testing Techniques*

[48] Beizer, Boris [1995], *Black Box Testing*

[49] Myers, Glenford [1979] *The Art of Software Testing*

PART II

THIS IS THE main body of the book, and deals with how you develop good test cases well. The test design techniques described are all usable in practice, and supplement each other. The theories behind the techniques are described thoroughly, and each technique is demonstrated with the help of examples that you can follow step by step. The most important ones also include exercises. Being able to use the techniques is the first step: knowing how to adapt them to your particular project is a skill which will come the more you work with them.

You will often end up in situations where you have to adapt the techniques described, or use other techniques in order to solve your problems. You are welcome to share these experiences with the author for future editions of this book.

8 THE OVERARCHING PROCESS OF TEST DESIGN

FINALLY, WE NOW come to the most exciting part of test work: building test cases. Since test design is complicated, and contains many different approaches, it is appropriate to divide the work up into several steps. It rapidly becomes complicated if you try to combine flows, test data and complicated combinations of parameters at one and the same time. You end up with a large and often incomplete picture which is impractical to work with. The test design process described is a practical and structured way of working and is well tried out in practice. Most of the techniques described in this book contain the first three steps and, some, all four.

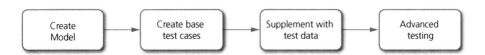

Figure 8.1: Process for test design in four steps. We start with an analysis of the test basis and creation of a model. Then we cover the model, supplement it with test data, and end with the advanced testing which is perhaps not always covered by the model.

8.1 Preparation – Get the Big Picture

Before you begin to develop test cases, it is a good idea to compile an overview of what is to be tested. Often, the test strategy contains some form of overview of the test coverage. Find out which documents and other test basis are available to you to work from. This can be anything from business plans to technical models and program specifications with database descriptions. Go through the test basis and try to identify which requirements you are affected by. If the requirements are not written down, you need to conduct a dialogue with those placing the order, and the developer, in order to obtain the test basis you need. All the requirements we have identified, and all the requirements we can assume exist, even if they are not written down, must now be tested. As a test designer, you must find a way of arriving at the right questions to ask.

8.2 Step One – Creating a Model of the Requirements

When the overview is complete, it is time to build test cases. Your first step is to model the requirements in a form which you will cover by test cases in the next step. As I have described before, there are many types of model to use and, in the majority of projects, you must use several different types in order to give as good a variation as possible to the test cases. Common models are tables, flow graphs and state diagrams.

Remember that you must have early involvement in the project. You must develop your models in parallel with the requirements being written. By compiling the models, you will contribute to the quality assurance of both the requirements and the design. Here, you have the opportunity to contribute genuinely to the common good, by asking important questions at such an early stage that they can be answered in time before the coding gets under way. On the other hand, do not try to develop all your test cases in detail before you have had your models examined and accepted by the rest of the project team. It is obviously a good thing to think like a tester and question almost everything, but do not be too hard in your criticism, since your job is to be an asset to the project team, and not to run down the other team members. Do it right and you will be appreciated for your competence and for what you contribute. What you actually do is the part known as analysis in many project models, which often contains the steps requirements-analysis-design-coding-testing. It can be argued that those who compile the requirements, or those who design the system, should carry out this analysis but, in my experience, this is seldom the case. Also, even if those who write the requirements, or design the system, carry out this analysis, they do not ask the same questions as you do as a tester.

8.3   Step Two – Covering the Model, Creating Base Test Cases

Step two is to cover the model with test cases. In this way, you get a measure of which test coverage you have. Graphic models are filled in through writing test cases which encompass all the rectangles and circles in place, and the arrows linking them up. For formulae or sets of rules, it is a question of all the parameters involved being tested, as well as the most important combinations of them.

For practical reasons, we choose, in this situation, to postpone the compiling of precise test data. It is simpler to deal with one issue at a time. The test cases you now generate, which contain flows, combinations of variables or conditions, but no precise data, are what we call base test cases, in order to emphasise that this is only the first step.

8.4   Step Three – Supplementing With Test Data

The base test cases we have generated in step two must now be run once or several times with different data in order to achieve a greater depth of testing.

Equivalence partitioning of each parameter and boundary value analysis provides you with relevant values for dividing up the test data. When you have several different variables which work together, it is not enough to analyse the variables one by one, but also in combination with each other.

8.5   Step Four – Advanced Testing

Finally, combinations of test cases and data come in a more advanced form. It is a matter of combinations of test cases, unusual assumptions and actual change in the system. Apart from the fact that many of our techniques have a fourth step, there are also special techniques and approaches for advanced testing. Examples of this are:

– cyclical tests – (data cycles, time cycles)
– several test cases run together – (parallelity etc.)
– exploratory testing – (ideas which are difficult to think of in advance)
– scenario testing – (how will it look in reality?)
– soap opera testing – (all the strange and extreme combinations you can think of, and then more still)

Here, the test cases are packaged and pieced together in chains, if they are to be run in a particular order. See chapter 22.

9 MODELS

What do you do if you see a model? – Cover it.[50]

To be able to handle complex reality, science has always worked to simplify it into a more manageable form. A picture of a hydrogen atom is often drawn as a proton like a cannonball in the middle, and an electron on a circle around it. This is remote from reality, where the electron is to be found inside some sort of cloud around the centre. However, the advantage of this is that the model of the atom helps us to understand different chemical reactions and characteristics of hydrogen.[51] At the other end of the scale is the globe, which can be used to explain the picture of the world we have today, namely that the Earth is round. We can also understand why it is night on the one side, and day on the other, if we shine a lamp on the globe and spin it around.

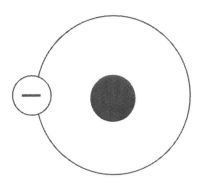 

Figure 9.1 Two models on a completely different level and scale. Both are simplifications, but are still extremely useful for understanding things like chemical reactions or time zones.

When I travel to a city for the first time as a tourist, the first thing I do is to get hold of a map of the city. The map is extremely different from the city itself. There is neither asphalt, nor any cobble stones, just black lines of varying thickness which mean «here is a street». We have created an extremely simplified model which, in all its simplicity, helps us to succeed in our quest for sightseeing attractions. This suits our purposes, and most of us understand it with a little practice. Had the model been too simple, we would not have seen the difference between a cycle path and a highway, and it would have been difficult for us to drive in the city. Had the map been more detailed, it would have been difficult to decipher for the average tourist. An orienteering map, on the other hand, is significantly more detailed, and has both contour lines and individual large rock formations marked out in order to be better suited in that context.

Different models, with varying degrees of detail, suit different aims, but no model is a perfect depiction of reality. Actually, the only thing we can say about a model, is that it is incomplete and, probably, not entirely correct!

We do precisely the same thing in test design: we create models of our reality which make it possible for us to work effectively on developing suitable test cases. It is important to differentiate between the model we are creating and the reality it represents. If we create a model which poorly describes the system we are to test, our test cases will be inferior for it. Absolutely one of the most important characteristics in a skilful tester is the ability to generate good models of the reality we are to test. It is a matter for us to generate models which stand up to scrutiny.[52]

Our models can be in the form of tables, flowcharts or other graphs which describe how the system works. When we have compiled models, we can then apply the relevant techniques in order to achieve good test cases with good coverage. This book describes a number of ways of modelling real problems, and different techniques available for creating test cases out of the models. All models have been used in real situations and the majority of examples and exercises come from projects where the author, or a colleague, has personally taken part.

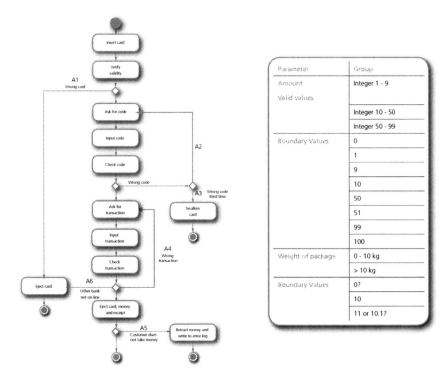

Insert card
Verify validity
A1 — Wrong card
Ask for code
Input code
A2
Check code
Wrong code
A3 — Wrong code third time
Ask for transaction
Swallow card
Input transaction
A4 — Wrong transaction
Check transaction
A6 — Other bank not on-line
Eject card
Eject card, money and receipt
A5 — Customer does not take money
Retract money and write to error log

And a table for test data:

Parameter	Group
Amount	Integer 1 - 9
Valid values	
	Integer 10 - 50
	Integer 50 - 99
Boundary Values	0
	1
	9
	10
	50
	51
	99
	100
Weight of package	0 - 10 kg
	> 10 kg
Boundary Values	0?
	10
	11 or 10.1?

Figure 9.2: Two models for test design, a flowchart and a table for test data. These are also simplifications, but they still help us to develop better test cases.

FOOTNOTES

[50] Beizer, Boris[1995], *Black Box Testing* p.31

[51] Weinberg, Gerald[2001]: *An Introduction to General Systems Thinking*, Chapter 1

[52] Bach, James [2005]: *Rapid Testing course material.*

10 EQUIVALENCE PARTITIONS AND BOUNDARY VALUES

EQUIVALENCE PARTITIONING IS intended for reducing the total number of tests by grouping together data or test cases which test the same thing, and then making do with testing one value out of each group. The idea is that, if you expect the same result from two tests, it is sufficient to run one of them. A group of tests are equivalent if:

- They test the same thing
- If one of them detects a defect, the other one will probably do so as well
- If one of them does not detect a defect, neither will the other one

These ideas apply to all types of test but, in this chapter, we are working specifically with test data.[53] The experience gained shows that defects often crop up on or precisely across the boundary values. This applies to both input and output data. The step after you compile the groups involves choosing values on and around the boundaries of each group. The recommendation for how many values you should choose varies according to whom you ask, but it is usually two or three values per boundary. For numerical intervals, it is natural to detect boundary values. For other types of group, it is not as easy – often there are no boundary values.

Equivalence partitions and boundary value analysis are primarily about how we compile good test data, and are used in step three in the test design process.

10.1 Numerical Values
Numerical variables often have values in coherent intervals. These have both valid and invalid groups and boundary values.

10.1.1 Equivalence Partitions
Example on book ordering: When you order books on the internet, the number of books ordered is fed in as a positive integer between 1 and 99. It is natural to assume that the system handles all numbers from 1 to 99 in a similar way – if it works for one of these values, it presumably works for all the others. Then, you will want to cover all the values which lie above and below the valid interval – hence the two other groups. We therefore have one valid group, all integers from 1 to 99, and two invalid ones, all integers <1 and integers >99. A tabular description of this might look as follows:

Parameter	Group
Amount	Integer 1 - 99
Valid values	
Amount	Integer < 1
Invalid values	Integer > 99

Figure 10.1: Table of valid groups for the quantity parameter. The principle is that it is sufficient to test one value in each group.

If we then begin to think about all the possibilities available for feeding in invalid values, the number of invalid groups grows rapidly. There is nothing to say that you have to test all the different invalid values. It may be sufficient to have a single group of invalid values – it depends on how accurate you wish to be. So that the example becomes clearer, we will choose to divide the invalid values into several groups. As we can see, there are often significantly more invalid intervals than there are valid ones. Granted, if you judge it necessary, you can both group together different and often invalid intervals, or divide them up into several parts. There is no absolute rule for how you should go about it. This rather varies from case to case, largely dependent on the logic in the program.

Parameter	Group
Amount Valid values	Integer 1 - 99
Amount Invalid values	Integer < 1
	Integer > 99
	Decimal number 1.01 - 99.99
	Letters
	+, - ,*
	Calculation operators
	Other non - numerical symbols
	Empty field

Figure 10.2: Table of valid and invalid groups for the quantity parameter.

ESSENTIAL SOFTWARE TEST DESIGN

10.1.2 Boundary Values

Numerical parameters also have both valid and invalid boundary values.

Parameter	Boundary value
Amount	1
Valid values	99
Amount	0
Invalid values	100

Figure 10.3: Table of boundary values for the quantity parameter by groups already developed.

A graphical description of those values which are integers is in the diagram below.

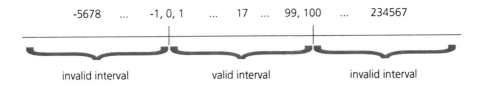

Figure 10.4: Equivalence partitions and boundary values for number of books, drawn on a scale. Here, we can see how, with a few values, we can cover a large area.

10.1.3 More Factors Affecting Grouping

There may be rules which give you more groups than the ones above. The valid grouping 1–99 might have to be divided up into more subgroups. One example may be where you get a discount if you order at least 10 copies of the same book, and an even larger one if you order at least 51. Another may be where you get free delivery, but only up to a package weight of 10 kilograms. All of a sudden, you have more groups and an extra parameter in the form of weight. The number of boundary values grows at the same time by at least two per new interval. In practice, every rule can give us different divisions of data. That means that step three in the test design process, supplementing test data, must be considered for all the base test cases we compile.

Parameter	Group
Amount Valid values	Integer 1 - 9
	Integer 10 - 50
	Integer 50 - 99
Boundary Values	0
	1
	9
	10
	50
	51
	99
	100
Weight of package	0 - 10 kg
	> 10 kg
Boundary Values	0?
	10
	11 or 10.1?

Figure 10.5: Expanded table of valid and invalid groups for the quantity parameter. When there are rules giving you more groups.

10.1.4 Open Boundaries

In some cases, there are no boundaries defined for a value. This can apply to e.g. a person's age – how old can you be and still have a bank account or receive payments through your pension? The following guidelines are suggested in these cases:[54]

- Discuss requirement or design specification in order to check whether there really is no boundary – sometimes there are boundaries even though they are not written down
- Set a fictional boundary which is doubtlessly beyond a realistic maximum value (e.g. a human can live to 120 years)
- Research technical limitations – for example, the size of an input field or database
- Look for boundaries in the rest of the system, or systems you communicate with

ESSENTIAL SOFTWARE TEST DESIGN

10.2   Values with Shared Characteristics

Certain variables can be grouped together according to their characteristics, or which output data they are expected to generate. For example, you can divide months into groups according to the number of days in them.

Parameter	Groups
Months	January, March, May, July, August, October, December
Valid values	April, June, September, November
	February
Months	»All other values«
Invalid values	

Figure 10.6 Table of groups for the Month parameter

All countries in the world can be seen as a group, where all objects are treated equally. However, depending on the application, they can also be divided up into groups according to which continent they are in.

Example on book ordering: For our web store, orders from the UK attract free delivery, while people ordering in other countries in Europe pay a fixed price, and the rest of the world, a higher price. To achieve the correct division, you have to know the logic behind the handling method. Even the way you input the country matters – if we assume that the country is chosen manually from a list on the screen, there is a limit to the possibilities of choosing the wrong value – there is nothing to say that you can write anything into the field.

Example on Countries:

Parameter	Groups
Country	England, Northern Ireland, Scotland, Wales
Valid values	Other European countries
	Rest of the World
Country	Empty field
Invalid values	
	»All other values« (perhaps not possible – try anyway!)

Figure 10.7 Table of groups for the Country parameter. Grouping is by what we require as regards postage price, in other words, output data.

Here there are no obvious boundary values. In some cases, depending on the program logic, you can find values which are specific to each case. To choose a country, we can see the first and last country in the list as boundary values. However, you often choose to regard lists as intervals without boundary values. One possible solution is to set boundary values, but to give them a lower priority.

Payment on the internet can be made by invoice, by feeding in a VISA card number, Mastercard number, or specifying cash on delivery – if we prescribe that all card payments are made in the same way, we get the subdivision below. Here you can discuss whether the different types of card are to be handled separately – the answer is that it depends on the program. For form of payment, there are no boundary values.

Parameter	Groups
Form of payment	Invoice
Valid values	VISA, MasterCard
	Cash on delivery
Form of payment	Empty field
Invalid values	Other value?

Figure 10.8 Table of groups for the Form of Payment parameter. Sometimes, there is only one value in each group, which depends on the fact that we want to test all the variants in existence.

10.3 Text Fields

Text fields are variables where you can write in a large number of values which do not always fit together. There are annotation fields, where you can type in pieces of text or calculations, including formatting and line breaks. Other variables are shorter and can be subject to a format restriction.

Example: Surname of maximum 20 characters

Parameter	Groups
Name (20)	1 - 20 characters
Valid values	a - z, A - Z
	å,ä,ö, Å,Ä,Ö
	1 - 20 characters af, de, space O'Connor, double barrel etc.
Name	Empty field (can be permitted)
Invalid values	> 20 characters
	Other characters not allowed in name e.g, @, +,?

Figure 10.9 Table of groups for the Surname parameter. Text fields can be complicated to test, since the possible variants are infinite. Swedish characters are tested especially carefully since they often give rise to problems.

The special Swedish characters (å, ä and ö) are always problematic and should be tested especially carefully, because they sit in their own group. Also, in this case, you should question whether twenty characters is sufficient to handle all surnames. Here, there are both valid and invalid boundary values.

Parameter	Group
Name (20)	1 character, a - ö
Valid boundary values	20 characters, a - ö
Name	0 characters -
Invalid values	Already marked as an invalid group – write only in one place!
	21 characters

Figure 10.10 Table of boundary values for the Surname parameter. Both the number of characters, and the value set have boundary values.

If we look at the list of ASCII characters below (apart from the first special characters, Page Break, New Line etc.), we can see that the boundary values for numerical fields can be / and :. Besides this, we can see why å, ä and ö are more complicated to handle, since they sit apart from the rest of the alphabet. If I see Torbj}rn anywhere in the interface, I know what the cause is.

!"#$%&'()*+,./0123456789:;<=>?@ABCDEFGHIJKLMNOPQRSTUVWXYZ[\
]^_`abcdefghijklmnopqrstuvwxyz{|}~ ‚ƒ„…†‡ˆ‰Š‹Œ Ž   ''""•——˜™š›œ
žŸ ¡¢£¤¥¦§¨©ª«¬®¯°±²³´µ¶·¸¹º»¼½¾¿ÀÁÂÃÄÅÆÇÈÉÊËÌÍÎÏÐÑÒÓÔÕÖ×ØÙÚ
ÛÜÝÞßàáâãäåæçèéêëìíîïðñòóôõö÷øùúûüýþÿ

Figure 10.11: ASCII characters Nos. 32 to 255. We can see why there can be a problem with Swedish characters being spread about, and not in sequence with the other characters.

We might consider solving the problem with the large variation in surnames by accepting any kind of input. Since it is difficult to decide what constitutes valid combinations, we record what is input without any checks. Then, all the processing is left to mechanisms like the database processor deeper inside the system. The risk is that problems will arise where the information has to be saved in the database, which perhaps cannot handle just any kind of information. Also, if you manage to save it, the information is most often used later by other parts of the system, where defects can arise because of a lack of input data checking earlier on.

10.4 Time Dependent Variables

Here, it is a matter of when you carry out a test in relation to another event which depends on time. Take an example, like sending to a printer. Here, you can choose to print when the printer is free, while it is printing something else or precisely when it has finished with another printout. The same way of thinking is used when it comes to database communication.

Parameter	Groups
Time	Vacant printer
Valid values	Busy printer
Time	Printer not connected
Invalid values	Printer disconnected while in use

Figure 10.12 Table of time-dependent groups for printer jobs.

Boundary values for the printer are:

Parameter	Groups
Time Valid boundary values	Just before or after completed print job
Time Invalid boundary values	Is there one?

Figure 10.13 Table of time-dependent boundary values for printer jobs.

10.5 Logical Values

There are choice boxes where you choose Yes/No or Checked/Empty. These can sometimes have an extra value which denotes that no choice has been made – greyed out. In the database it may appear as Y/N/(blank) or 1/o/(blank).

Parameter	Groups
Check-box Valid values	Yes
	No
	Greyed out
Check-box Invalid values	Not Chosen (can be valid or invalid depending on whether the field is mandatory or not)

Figure 10.14 Table of groups for logical parameters. Yes, No or Not Chosen are the only values available.

10.6 Relationships Between Fields

In certain cases the value set is governed in one field, and the value in another field. In these cases you have no absolute boundary values, but relative ones. To know what to test, you need relative subdivisions.

Parameter	Groups
Withdrawal from account	Withdrawal ≤ balance on account
Valid values	Withdrawal > balance on account
Withdrawal from account	Withdrawal > maximum withdrawal from account
Invalid values	

Figure 10.15 Table of groups for parameters dependent on other parameters. Permitted withdrawal depends upon the balance in the account.

Boundary values exist if relationships are an interval.

Parameter	Groups
Withdrawal from account	Withdrawal 1 SEK
Valid boundary values	Withdrawal balance on account +1 SEK
Withdrawal from account	Withdrawal maximum withdrawal from account +1 SEK
Invalid boundary values	

Figure 10.16 Table of boundary values for parameters dependent on other parameters

There is nothing to say that a relative dependency is always an interval. There are also logical relationships which only have the variations Yes or No. Then, it is actually a matter of the set of rules we use, for example, using the decision tables technique.

10.7 Sequences with Values

There are examples of parameters where each value is dealt with in a unique way. In this case, each value becomes its own interval. These can be alternatives on a menu, a list of valid airport codes or currency codes.

Parameter	Groups
Airport code	All valid designations used
Valid values	Valid designations which may not be used for some reason
Airport code	All other letter combinations which do not exist
Invalid values	Empty field
	Invalid values

Figure 10.17 Table of groups of value sequences. Here, it is not clear whether there is more than one group.

Here, the actual boundary value is missing. You might be able to choose to have the first or last alternative in a list as the boundary values if you want to be particularly accurate.

Parameter	Groups
Airport code	First valid code
Valid values	Last valid code
Airport code	Missing
Invalid values	

Figure 10.18 Table of possible boundary values for value sequences. There is a risk, albeit a small one, that the first and last values can produce defects.

10.8   Combined List on the Example of Book Ordering

If we put together the whole list of parameters in our example, we get the summary below:

Parameter	Group
Amount Valid values	Integer 1 - 99
Amount Invalid values	Integer < 1
	Integer > 99
	Decimal number 1.01 - 99.99
	Letters
	+, -, .*
	calculation operators
	Other non - numerical symbols
	Empty field
Country Valid values	England, Northern Ireland, Scotland, Wales
	Other European countries
	Rest of the World
Country Invalid values	Empty field
	»All other values« (perhaps not possible – try anyway!)
Form of payment Valid values	Invoice
	VISA. MasterCard
	Cash on delivery
Form of payment Invalid values	Empty field

Figure 10.19 Combined table for the parameters in the book ordering example. In the table, we can combine several different values in the same test case.

10.9 Fuzzy Groups

In certain cases, it can be very difficult to divide variables into intervals. For example, take the testing of web applications which have to work on different operating systems and different web browsers installed in different languages. How do we split these up into groups? In principle, every configuration (operating system, web application language) is unique in its own way. The answer is that, in this case, you have to try to make a judgement about which configurations can be regarded as equivalent. In this case, there is a greater risk that you miss defects that are dependent on a certain combination of variables. It is often a very subjective judgement but, in any case, better than not trying at all.

The same applies to printouts which have to work on the most common printers – do you divide on the basis of brand or type?

10.10 Domain Tests

The situation where several different variables work together, and have to be tested together, is often called *domain testing*. The principle is the same as before, with the difference that there are several different variables which, together, define the groups.

Later in this book, we will deal with the decision table and decision tree techniques. There, we divide up all customers according to a large number of rules, where each rule is dependent on several different variables. An ingenious aspect in the set of rules is the way of grouping, for example, rules 3,4,6 and 7 in the table below.

Tabell 10.20

Rule	Age	Liability order	Capital loss previous year	Income previous year	Income/age
1		No	≤ 100		
2	≤ 42	No	> 100	≤ 120	
3	≤ 42	No	> 100, ≤ 426	> 120	≤ 50
4	≤ 42	No	> 100	> 120	> 75
5	> 42	No	> 100		
6	≤ 42	No	> 100, ≤ 426	> 120	> 50, ≤ 75
7	≤ 42	No	> 426	> 120	≤ 75
8		Yes			

Figure 10.20 Decision table for the parameters in the book ordering example. Domain tests are used when the groups consist of several different variables that work together.

When we have two parameters that are mutually dependent, it is relatively simple to describe graphically but, if there are more, we have to use another method. If we draw up the rules on a diagram with regard to the parameters *Capital loss in the previous year* and *Income/Age quotient* we get the following picture:

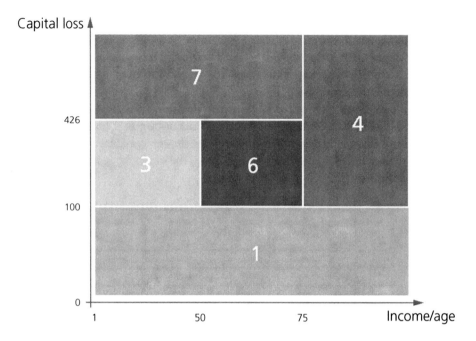

Figure 10.21: Diagram showing graphically domain tests where more than one parameter governs groups and boundary values.

Here, there are boundary values along each line divided between two fields. Especially important are the ones which lie on an intersection between three or more rules. It speaks for itself that we cannot test all values alongside all common boundary values. If we now simplify further, we can choose those values where at least three lines meet, wherever that may be. We end up with the table below.

ESSENTIAL SOFTWARE TEST DESIGN

	Income/age	Capital loss
Rule 1	0	0
	0	100
	50	100
	51	100
	75	100
	76	100
	Max	0
	Max	100
Rule 3	0	101
	0	426
	50	101
	50	426
Rule 4	76	101
	76	Max
	Max	101
	Max	Max
Rule 6	51	101
	51	426
	75	101
	75	426
Rule 7	0	427
	0	Max
	75	427
	75	Max

Figure 10.22: Table showing boundary values from the Domain Tests diagram, where more than one parameter governs groups and boundary values. There are boundary values in every place where one or more lines end.

10.11 Tips for Equivalence Partitioning

- Do not forget to group with regard to results/output data – which input data can result in a certain output – and both valid and invalid values
- Study the logic in the program you are to test – this is what determines what the groupings are
- Equivalence partitions are an excellent aid to compiling test data, but the principle applies to all types of test

- You can certainly combine values from several valid groups in the same test case.
- Avoid combining several invalid values, where the first «error» can stop the execution and prevent the other values from being tested
- If you want to test whether the program can handle several errors at the same time, you must include several invalid values in the same test case
- Boundary value analysis is an excellent aid to compiling test data

10.12 Template and Example

With this template, you can pick out test cases and test data. Each column is a test case.

Description								
Parameter	Value	1	2	3	4	5	6	7
Amount · Valid groups	Integer 1 - 99	X			X	X		
Invalid groups	Integer < 1							
	Integer > 99						X	
	Decimal number 1.01 - 99.99							
	Letters							
	+, - ,*							
	Calculation operators							
	Other non - numerical symbols							
Amount · Valid boundary values	1			X				
	99		X					
Amount · Invalid boundary values	0							
	100							
Country – groups	England, Northern Ireland, Scotland, Wales		X					
	Other European countries	X					X	
	Rest of the World			X				
Country – boundary values	First country in the list				X			
	Last country in the list					X		
Form of payment – groups	Invoice	X				X		
	VISA, MasterCard			X	X			
	Cash on delivery		X				X	

Figure 10.23: Template for developing equivalence partitions and boundary values: check the combinations you want in each test case

You can also write the values directly into the table

Description								
Parameter	Value	1	2	3	4	5	6	7
Amount - Valid groups	Integer 1 - 99	4						
Amount - Invalid groups	Integer < 1						- 4	
	Integer > 99						111	
	Decimal number 1.01 - 99.99						1.5	
	Letters						Ff	
	+, -, * calculation operators						1	
	Other non - numerical symbols						@	
Amount - Valid boundary values	1			1				
	2					2		
	98				98			
	99		99					
Amount - Invalid boundary values	0						0	
	100							
Country - groups	England, Northern Ireland, Scotland, Wales		NI					
	Other European countries	SE					FI	
	Rest of the World			US				
Country - boundary values	First country in the list				A			
	Last country in the list					Ö		
Form of payment - groups	Invoice	Yes						
	VISA, MasterCard		Visa	MC				
	Cash on delivery							

Figure 10.24: Template and example for developing equivalence partitions and boundary values, writing data directly into the table

I often use the matrix above for compiling and documenting test data. If the data are complex, I divide it up into several smaller tables.

Obviously, it is also possible to use the model above as documentation during the execution of tests, and to write in values and results afterwards. This is especially useful for detailed tests of a particular function, and for component tests. In this way, test cases and results are in the same place and can easily be surveyed and updated.

FOOTNOTES

[53] Myers, Glenford [1979] *The Art of Software Testing*, pp. 45–50

[54] Grove Consultants [2002]: *Test Practitioner course material*

11 TESTING BUSINESS PROCESSES

THE OVERARCHING PROCESSES in a company are often called business processes. In a use case-driven project, they are documented as *Business Use Cases*. During the greater part of a project, we focus on individual functions or areas of function but, also, we must not forget to check that the overarching processes work.

Start from the operation's method described in a work flow. All manual routines, user handbooks and paper materials are included. It is important to remember who performs each part, and what permissions that person should have. If the flow does not already exist in the form of a graph, it is appropriate to compile it. Ensure that you have thought the model through correctly, by discussing it with appropriate business personnel. One useful method for developing actual use with variants, is to make use of different *personas* for the users in mind. A *Persona* is defined as: *«a precise description of the user, what he or she will achieve and why»* in the excellent book *About Face*[55]. The method caters mostly for designers and architects, but is also useful for test design.

We assume that the inherent operational sub processes have already been tested and work as intended. The testing of business processes verifies the connection between the manual and the automatic sub processes. The following are usual sub processes:[56]

1. Are the assumptions for each step fulfilled?
2. Is there enough information in the automated system for the next manual step to be executable, and vice versa?
3. Most often, several different people or roles are involved, and then it is a matter of every person having the right access to those functions they are to carry out, but no more than they are permitted.
4. Is there a user handbook, help function or are there other usability aspects?
5. Information communicated to customers, and received by us from customers, has to be checked.
6. It is common for the processes to be walked through as a form of role-playing, with the aid of both paper material and system support.

11.1 The Model

Often, there is only a text description but, sometimes, there is a simple flow graph. I prefer to generate my own model from the requirements, consisting of one flow, since the information available is seldom good enough for testing.

Example: Handling sickness notification for the Swedish Industrial and Commercial Supplementary Pension (Industrins och Handelns Tilläggspension, ITP):

1. A sickness notification for an insurance policy holder is received.
2. The operator checks which types of insurance are registered in different systems.
3. Decisions on payment are made, and a form is sent out requesting tax details, form of payment and account number.
4. The policy holder replies with answers to these questions.
5. Payment takes place to the specified account.
6. Every three months, a request for a doctor's note is sent out.
7. The policy holder replies with the doctor's note.
8. When the recovery notification is issued, the total amount paid out is calculated and any necessary reimbursement request is sent out.
9. The job is complete when the final debt is settled.

Here, the flow is written in a purely linear form, which is not really correct. A more detailed analysis of the text gives us the following graph. The next step is to discuss the graph you have drawn up with somebody responsible for operations, in order to obtain confirmation that it is right. Often, a whole host of supplementary information arises from this work.

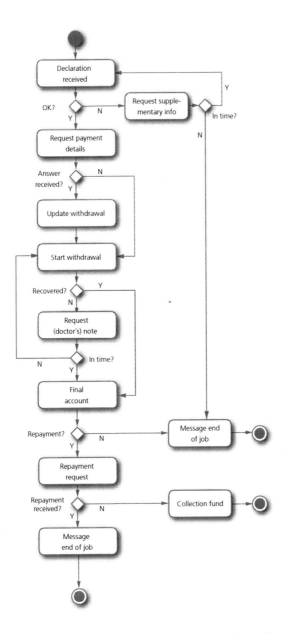

Figure 11.1: Flowchart description of business process for sickness notification. If we draw in all the different variations which can occur, it becomes easier to arrive at the right test case. At the same time, it is an important way of quality assuring the requirements.

11.2 Base Test Case

Once you have arrived at a graph which has been approved by the operations staff, you can generate your test cases. To compile these, you compile the different routes through the graph. Think about what different users there are, and how they will be using the system. Start with the most common flows, and then consider all the variants, and what can go wrong at every given moment.

From the graph above, you end up with the following base test case: there are more variants than this, but I consider that these will do to start with. Only the first case is described in all its steps, the others only by the headings:

Test Case 1: Ill for two months (the whole flow)
1. Notification received and correct. Policy holder is in the system.
2. Request for payment details sent out.
3. Reply with account number and tax details received in time, details entered into the system.
4. Payment begins.
5. Recovered after two months.
6. Final calculation shows that sickness benefit has been paid out for one week too many.
7. Repayment request is sent out.
8. Repayment received in time.

Test Case 2: Supplementary information required. Answers to payment detail request received late. First payment on payment card. Subsequent payments on account. No repayment.
Comment: this was one variant not in the graph. Discuss whether the graph needs to be updated with new information, or whether this would make it too complex. Not all details need to be in the graph.

Test Case 3: Supplementary information requested but is not received in time. The job is completed without any payment of benefit.

Test Case 4: Completion of job without benefit payment requirement.

11.3 Test Data

Identify the different variables which can influence how the process works: this applies especially to the question of which permissions people need to have in order to carry out their duties; remember that they should have permissions neither too extensive, nor too limited. Test data are developed with the help of equivalence partitions and boundary value analysis.

Often, there is test data already compiled earlier on in the more detailed test cases. Our aim in this case is, Mainly, to check the different flows, and not all variations of the test data. This, we assume, has been tested earlier. A table of test data may look like the one below:

Parameter	Group	TF1 a	TF1 b	TF2 a
Operator's permissions	Correct	X	X	X
	Not enough			
	Too large			
Number of insurance policies	Missing			
	System A	X		
	System B		X	
	System C		X	X
	Exists in several different systems		X	
Withdrawal details				
Tax	0,3	X		X
	Table		X	X
	0% - adjustment			
	100% - Adjustment			
Amount	< 50 kr			
	50 - max	X	X	X
	Invalid values			
Payment to	Bank account	X	X	X
	Withdrawal card			X
Periods of illness	1	X	X	
	Several			X
Repayment	0 (no)			X
	< 2000	X		
	≥ 2000		X	

Figure 11.2: Table of test data for the business process Sickness Notification. We focus on the variables controlling the flow, and not on the extremity values.

We can then generate the test cases by putting crosses in the table. Obviously, it is a good thing to have variations on the test data, even if we are working at a more overarching level, where flows, access to the system, mail-outs to the customer and user management are in our focus.

11.4 Advanced Testing

Finally, we put the sub processes together in their context. In our case, with sickness insurance, this means, for example:

1. That a number of different policy holders are created within the system.
2. That these then work for a certain period, and premiums are paid in.
3. Then, a sickness notification for a certain length of time is received.
4. One of them has several disconnected periods of sickness.
5. Another becomes liable for repayments.
6. Etc.

For this more advanced procedure, you can use the supplementary techniques scenario-based testing and soap-opera testing. It might be a good idea to use a test charter to describe the test cases.

Theme	You are the admin of HR for the central database in Sweden. Your task is to set-up all of the base-variables that will be used by every country. Next task is to set-up the local managers for Sweden so the system can be configured locally. Perform all checks and back-ups.
Setup	Assure that your admin account(s) are set up with rights to configure all tables. Also make sure that the environment is set-up correctly.
Activities	☐ Go to central panel and do set-up ☐ Set-up all local variables for Sweden
Oracle Notes	View updated central tables to verify they have been updated properly. View updated local tables to verify they are correct. Verify that you can use the settings to add one employee.
Variations	USER DATA: Restrict the rights of the user account to the maximum degree while still being able to perform the activity. Can you take away admin privileges for the admin account. What happens then? TUG OF WAR: log in as a second admin user and try to update the same tables, or cancel updates; log in as the same user as if you forgot you already had another window open, then make changes in both windows. OOPS: update the wrong table and then undo the update INTERRUPTION: Try to make updates while a buffer update is going on... LIFECYCLE: Update a table, update it several more times, advancing the simulation date.

Figure 11.3: Example of a simple test charter that specifies what is to be tested but gives the tester a lot of creative freedom.

11.5 Testing with the Help of Prototypes

Prototypes are often used during the design of a system, but can also be successfully applied to testing. Prototypes are created in order to answer questions. Which type of question we want to ask determines which kind of prototype needs to be generated. Just because a question is difficult and intricate to answer, does not mean that the prototype itself needs to be complicated.[57]

A general distinction which is usually made is between lo-fi and hi-fi prototypes. By lo-fi prototypes, what is meant are simple, paper-based prototypes which are a long way from being complete systems, while hi-fi prototypes are often computer-based and more realistic. Lo-fi prototypes are most often used to test content, and logic in the work flow, without getting bogged down in the detail. Hi-fi prototypes are more appropriate for testing how the system works in practice, and the graphical profile.

One colleague tells me that they perform the following test with the help of a lo-fi prototype:

Early on in the project, we run a dialogue check on how usable the functionality of the interface is, by running a number of scenarios with the aid of dialogue drawings in paper format. Defects, deficiencies and comments are noted. These are analysed and logged as defects. Here, we detect deficiencies before they are coded.

FOOTNOTES

[55] Cooper, Alan: *About Face 2.0* pp. 55–74
[56] PolPol, Martin, Ruud Teunissen, Erik van Veenendaal [2002] *Software Testing – A Guide to the TMAP Approach* p. 247
[57] Schrage, M. (1996) *Cultures of Prototyping in Winograd*, T. [ed.] (1996) *Bringing Design to Software* (Chapter 10), New York: Addison-Wesley.

12 FROM USE CASES TO TEST CASES

TO DESCRIBE THE requirements on a system, a technique is often used which is called use cases. We will not go into detail about exactly how these are written, since there is plenty of excellent material in this field. [58] [59] [60] If you have use cases as a basis, it is appropriate to use this technique, which builds on an analysis of the different flows at hand.

12.1 What are Use Cases?

Use cases are a step-by-step description of a flow, where an actor interact with a system. An actor may be one of a number of different user types, the system itself, or other external systems. It is usually said that a good use case should assign significant value to the actor. In other words, when the use case has been executed, the user has obtained a result which is of value to them. When, for example, *Withdraw Money* is complete, the actor has got their money in their hand. It can be a good idea to consider this when examining a use case, or starting test work based on a use case.

The commonest flow – normal use – is called the *main flow* (also called *the normal flow or Happy Path*) and variations of this are termed alternative flows. The level of detail is governed by whether it is the whole business process which has to be described, or selected parts of the overriding process. The assumptions, together with the actual actors, are specified and each flow has its final state described. This certainly sounds more or less like a well written test case.

A well-written use case is an excellent basis for writing test cases. With luck, the person who has written the use case has already generated an activity diagram which describes how the different flows fit together. In that case, your first step is to review the activity diagram from a test perspective. This step is very important from a quality assurance perspective and is developed in collaboration with requirement assessors and developers.

The overarching work procedure is this:
1. Compile an activity diagram. If this is already in place, the first step is to review it.
2. List all scenarios
3. Analyse and prioritise the scenarios according to risk – which are most important, commonest
4. Identify the operational variables which can affect the expected result
5. Write one or more test cases for each scenario

12.2 Use cases

Let us go back to the example of an ATM machine. A simple use case may look like this:

12.2.1 Example: Use Case – Withdraw Money
Assumptions

The customer's bank is one which is connected to the ATM system.

The customer has a correct and functioning magnetic strip card.

The ATM is switched on and is in ready mode.

The ATM is situated in Sweden so all withdrawals will be in swedish crowns, SEK, and bills that can be withdrawn are 100 or 500 only.

Actors

Customer

ATM (network)

Main Flow:

H-1.   The use case begins when the customer inserts the card.

H-2.   The ATM verifies the card and requests the PIN number.

H-3.   The customer types in the correct PIN (4 digits).

H-4.   The ATM verifies the PIN and asks the customer to type in an amount.

H-5.   The customer types in the amount (100-2000 SEK manually or by using the multiple choice keys).

H-6.   The ATM verifies that the amount is available in the customer's account and ejects the card, the money and the receipt, and registers the transaction in the customer's account.

H-7.   The customer takes the card, the money and the receipt.

H-8.   The ATM returns to standby mode.

H-9.   End of use case.

Results

The customer has carried out a successful withdrawal of money.

The customer's account is updated with the transaction.

Alternative Flows

Alternative flow – A1 Invalid card

A1-1.   At step H-1, the customer inserts an invalid card.

A1-2.   The ATM aborts the transaction and the card is ejected.

A1-3.   End of use case.

Alternative flow – A2 Wrong PIN
A2-1.   At step H-3, the customer types in the wrong PIN.
A2-2.   The ATM registers an incorrect PIN and asks the user to try again.
A2-3.   The use case continues with step H-3.

Alternative flow – A3 Wrong PIN, 3 times
A3-1.   At step H-3, the customer types in the wrong PIN three times in a row.
A3-2.   The ATM swallows the card and the transaction is aborted.
A3-3.   End of use case.

Alternative flow – A4 Incorrect input of amount
A4-1.   At step H-5, the customer makes an incorrect entry (not divisible by a hundred, funds are not in the account, exceeds permitted maximum withdrawal...)
A4-2.   The ATM disallows the entered amount and asks the user to try again.
A4-3.   The use case continues with step H-5.

Alternative flow – A5 Customer does not take the money
A5-1.   At step H-7, the customer takes the card, but not the money or the receipt within 20 seconds.
A5-2.   The ATM leaves the receipt hanging out of the machine and retracts the money, places it in a separate container and writes the amount, account number and cause of defect into a defect log.
A5-3.   The use case continues with step H-8.

Alternative flow – A6 The customer's bank is not on-line (other than Handelsbanken)
A6-1.   At step H-6, the ATM cannot verify whether the amount is available in the customer's account. A message shows that contact with the customer's bank is being established and the card is ejected.
A6-2.   The use case continues with step H-8.

Alternative flow – A7 Customer aborts the withdrawal
A7-1.   At all times in the Main flow, apart from steps H-6 and H-7, the customer can choose to abort the transaction
A7-2.   The ATM aborts the transaction and ejects the card, and no withdrawal

is recorded on the customer's account.

A7-3. The use case continues with step H-8.

12.3 The Model – Compiling the Flow Graph

If there is not one already, you compile a flow diagram based on the use case. Here, a notation format called UML is used – Unified Modelling Language – which is a *de facto* standard in IT today. [61] The picture below is called an activity diagram.

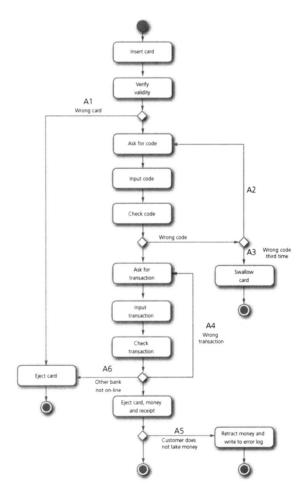

Figure 12.1: Activity diagram of the flow in the use case «Withdraw Money». We have a starting point but several different end points, with different results.

ESSENTIAL SOFTWARE TEST DESIGN

12.4 Creating Base Test Cases

12.4.1 List All Scenarios

To cover the graph, we generate base test cases for the different flows at hand

1. Start with the Main flow, which you use for the Happy Day test.
2. Continue with the alternative flows – one at a time.
3. There are different combinations of alternative flows. It is not always possible to draw up all the combinations: there may be infinite loops.

Scenario 1	Main Flow			
Scenario 2	Main Flow	A1		
Scenario 3	Main Flow	A2		
Scenario 4	Main Flow	A3		
Scenario 5	Main Flow	A4		
Scenario 6	Main Flow	A2	A2	A3
Scenario 7	Main Flow	A2	A4	
Scenario 8	Main Flow	A2	A2	A4
Etc.				

Figure 12.2: Table of scenarios for the flow in the use case «Withdraw Money». We can seldom cover all combinations of flows.

The Main flow is the most important one – it works at all times, and is used in the Happy Day test. Next, prioritise scenarios of alternative flows according to risk

- How important/critical they are
- How common they are

12.5 Supplement with Test Data

12.5.1 Identify Operational Variables

For each flow, find the parameters which influence how the use case is carried out. We call these the *operational variables*. In cases where the flow in the use case is long, or is affected by many variables, try to find a logical cut-off point and split up the flow into smaller parts. Obviously, it is the case that, for us to be able to run any tests at all, the customer and the account must exist in the system but, here, we are only walking through the variables controlling the flow in the use case.

Use a table in order to be able to find variations on how variables, on their own or together, can affect how a use case is carried out. The scenarios identified earlier are used as test basis in the table. Here, we have chosen to generate a table where each test case is a row, instead of a column as they were before. Obviously, it is also just as good to use the other variation of the table. Often, there is some sort of set of rules in the use case, or some other documentation (e.g. Supplementary Specification), which affects the result.

Scen ario	Prio	Card	PIN	With - drawal manual	With - drawal quick choice	Balance	Receipt	Type of notes in the ATM	ATM on - line	Expected result
		Governing variables								
1	1	OK	OK	OK	-	OK	OK	OK	OK	Withdrawal OK
2	2	Inv	-	-	-	-	-	-	OK	Error message, card ejected (no withdrawal)
3	2	OK	Inv	OK	-	OK	OK	OK	OK	Withdrawal OK, number of defective attempts set to zero

Figure 12.3: Table of the operational variables in the use case «Withdraw Money». It can be debated whether, for example, Name is a governing variable.

As we come by the operational variables, it quickly becomes apparent that, for example, Scenario 1 can be carried out in different ways with a satisfactory result.

Scen - ario	Prio	Card	PIN	With - drawal manual	With - drawal quick choice	Balance	Receipt	Type of notes in the ATM	ATM on - line	Expected result
		Operational variables								
1a	1	OK	OK	OK	-	OK	OK	OK	OK	Withdrawal OK
1b	1	OK	OK	-	OK	OK	OK	OK	OK	Withdrawal OK
1c	1	OK	OK	OK	-	OK	-	OK	OK	Withdrawal OK, no receipt
1d	1	OK	OK	-	OK	OK	-	500 notes only	OK	Withdrawal OK
1e	1	OK	OK	OK	-	OK	OK	100 notes only	OK	Withdrawal OK, no receipt

Figure 12.4: Table of possible variants of Scenario 1 for «Withdraw Money». Different assumptions mean that each base test case has to be run several times in order to achieve a good test.

12.5.2 Grouping Data

Appropriate test data are compiled, as usual, with the elementary techniques equivalence partitioning and boundary value analysis. Below is a table of the most important parameters, namely balance, withdrawal and card type.

Variable	Value
Balance – valid groups	Credit limit < balance < 0
	(if you have a credit)
	0 - 2000
	> 2000
Balance – invalid groups	Exceeded maximum credit?
Balance – valid boundary values	0
	2000
	Maximum in account?
	Credit limit
Balance – invalid boundary values	Credit limit – 1 SEK
Withdrawal – valid groups	Divisible by hundred 100 - 2000
Withdrawal – invalid groups	Divisible by hundred > 2000
	All numbers 100 - 2000 which are not divisible by 100
	Withdrawal which causes overdraft limit to be exceeded
Withdrawal – valid boundary values	100
	2000
	Withdrawal which causes exact overdraft limit to be reached
	Balance if less than 2000
Withdrawal – invalid boundary values	0
	2100
Card	Usual withdrawal card
	VISA
	MasterCard
	All credit cards
	Swedish bank
	Overseas bank
Cards – invalid	ICA, COOP, OK, Patient card
Restriction?	Valid card
	Restricted card

Figure 12.5: Table of test data for use case «Withdraw Money». Variants of test data require more test cases to be run.

Note that the grouping of test data for withdrawals can vary depending on the assumptions made. For example, what happens if there are only 500 SEK notes in the ATM?

12.5.3 Generate a Test Case for Each Scenario
The next step is to supplement our scenarios with identified test data.

Scenario	Prio	Operational variables								Expected result
		Card	PIN	Withdrawal manual	Withdrawal quick choice	Balance	Receipt	Type of notes in the ATM	ATM online	
1a	1	SHB	1234	100	-	100	OK	100 & 500 notes	OK	Withdrawal OK
1b	1	SHB	5678	-	700	1000	OK	100 & 500 notes	OK	Withdrawal OK
1c	1	SEB	9020	2000	-	2001	-	100 & 500 notes	OK	Withdrawal OK, no receipt
1d	1	Euro-Card	8520	-	1000	5230	-	Only 500	OK	Withdrawal OK
1e	1	FSB	7410	700	-	800	OK	Only 100	OK	Withdrawal OK, no receipt
2	2	Shell petrol card	-	-	-	-	-	-	OK	Error message, card ejected (no withdrawal)
3	2	Skandia-banken	Correct at 2nd attempt:	800	-	799	OK	100 & 500 notes	OK	Withdrawal OK, number of defective attempts set to zero
			4545			has credit				

Figure 12.6: Table of test cases with test data for the use case «Withdraw Money». From this table, it is possible to run the test cases directly without having to write anything else.

It is a good idea to cover all the important values and all the important flows, but it is impossible to cover all combinations. If we look at Scenario 1, the value *maximum withdrawal where the balance is less than 2000 SEK* is covered. We do not then necessarily need to have further tests for other base test cases where we test this boundary value.

12.6 Advanced Testing
In order to achieve really good tests, we have to think a little more broadly. In this case, it is appropriate to consider which different assumptions apply in order to withdraw money in a larger perspective..

Examples of advanced testing are:
- How much can a person take out per day/week/month/year?
- If the account is shared between more than one person, what applies then to withdrawal rules and PIN restrictions?
- What happens if the person before has typed in the wrong PIN: does it affect this withdrawal?
- Remember that, in most cases, there is an opportunity to abort what you are doing, at any point in the flow: this must also be tested. Most often, this is not written into a flow diagram, since the diagram is then in danger of becoming too complex.
- Different assumptions can produce different results in a test case. The system remembers what you did earlier. We have, firstly, inserted our card, typed the wrong code twice and then aborted the transaction. This produces other assumptions entirely than if, instead, we had continued the transaction and typed the correct code the third time. If we have these two different assumptions and then type the wrong code once, in the first case, the card will be swallowed by the machine and, in the second, we are clear to carry out the transaction.
- Remember that a real user will carry out several different scenarios through several different use cases. We must therefore also generate tests for expected actual use of the system, which involves several test cases in succession. This is a business process and, in a system where the end user does everything themselves, the assessment of the system will be judged on the whole. These tests also demonstrate more about usability as well as finding inconsistencies between use cases. Note that this must not be interpreted as though the use cases are placed in series. That method is not favoured by experts in use case modelling. Each use case must be capable of producing a value.
- Ideas about this can be obtained from an overview of the use case, and simple vision. Talking with domain experts applies here just as much as in all other forms of testing. Test suites for this type of testing can be generated out of other individual test cases for use cases. This is made easier if it is born in mind that the test cases must be suitable for combining when they

are designed. It is difficult to predict everything, but it is a good idea, for example, to use common test data from the very start.

12.7 Exercise

Start from the use case *Becoming a Customer* and compile test cases. As always, remember to question whether the requirements are correct and sufficient.

1. Compile or analyse activity diagrams for the flow and question whether they are correct.
2. Walkthrough together with the activity diagrams.
3. Identify operational variables and find variants.
4. Compile test cases for some of the scenarios.

12.7.1 Use case – AF001 Becoming a Customer
Short description
The use case describes how a customer is registered in the bank's Share Trading System for the first time. The customer has to undergo a credit check and is issued with an account number and a password which makes it possible to access the Share Trading System.

Actors
Potential Share Trading Customer, Bank Customer, Customer System, Credit Information Institute and Share Trading System

Assumptions
Potential Customer Share Trading is an existing Bank Customer. The customer has access to internet banking and has logged in to the system.

Main flow
H-1. The use case begins when the Potential Customer selects the application form to become a Customer of the Share Trading System.
H-2. The Share Trading System advises the Potential Customer that a credit check will take place during the application process.
H-3. The Potential Customer provides mandatory personal information: forename and surname, personal identification number, bank account number and signs the application electronically.
H-4. The Share Trading System checks whether the Potential Customer has provided the mandatory information and checks the information against the Customer System.

H-5. The Share Trading System confirms to the Potential Customer that the application is being processed.

H-6. The Share Trading System validates the Potential Customer by asking the Credit Information Institute if there are any official non-payment notices against their name.

H-7. The Credit Information Institute advises the Share Trading System that the Potential Customer has no official non-payment notices.

H-8. The Share Trading System approves the customer application and creates an account number and password for the account, which is printed out and sent by post. The Share Trading System explains to the Customer that the customer application has been approved, that the account number has been created and that the password is being sent by a letter in the post.

H-9. End of use case.

Results

A user profile is created for the Customer in the Share Trading System, together with an account number and password.

Alternative flow A1 – Potential Customer does not provide sufficient information

A1-1. At step H-4, the Share Trading System discovers that the Potential Customer has not provided mandatory information correctly.

A1-2. The Share Trading System informs the Potential Customer what is missing.

A1-3. The use case continues with step H-3.

Alternative flow A2 – Potential Customer has official non-payment notices.

A2-1. At step H-7 the Credit Information Institute informs the Share Trading System that the Potential Customer has official non-payment notices against their name.

A2-2. The Share Trading System saves the information that the application to become a customer has been rejected, together with the reason: official non-payment notice.

A2-3. The Share Trading System informs the Potential Customer that there are official non-payment notices against them and, therefore, the application cannot be approved.

A2-4. End of use case.

Alternative flow A3 – Credit Information Institute is not on-line

A3-1. At step H-6, the Share Trading System cannot establish contact with the Credit Information Institute.

A3-2. The Share Trading System informs the Potential Customer that their account number cannot be created, as no credit check can be performed at the moment.

A3-3. The Share Trading System updates the customer application with the cause of defect and asks the Potential Customer to try again later.

A3-4. The use case continues with step H-1.

Alternative flow A4 – Account Number cannot be created

A4-1. At step H-8, the Share Trading System fails to create an account number

A4-2. The Share Trading System informs the Potential Customer that an account number cannot be created.

A4-3. The Share Trading System updates the customer application with the cause of defect and asks the Potential Customer to try again later.

A4-4. The use case continues with step H-1.

Alternative flow A5 – Potential Customer chooses to abort

A5-1. At steps A3-4 and A4-4, the Potential Customer chooses to abort the application to become a customer.

A5-2. End of use case.

FOOTNOTES

[58] Leffingwell, Dean, Don Widrig[2003]: *Managing Software Requirements: A Use Case Approach* ISBN: 032112247X

[59] Robertson, Suzanne, James Robertson [1999]: *Mastering the Requirements Process* ISBN: 0201360462

[60] Schneider Geri, Jason Winters [2000]: *Applying Use Cases* ISBN 0-201-30981-5

[61] Fowler Martin, Kendall Scott [2003]: *UML Distilled: A Brief Guide to the Standard Object Modeling Language (Object Technology S.)* ISBN: 0321193687

13 STATE BASED TESTING

A STATE GRAPH, or *state transition testing*, is a model-based technique for compiling test cases. It works with event-driven systems, often in real time, and is common in areas like digital technology and electronics in hardware. The technique is very useful and has a large number of areas of use. Some examples of where I have used the technique myself are:

- Job processing systems, where each job goes through a number of different statuses, from when it is generated, to when it is completed
- Systems which have different states between which they switch, like ATM's and alcohol measuring devices
- Dialogues in graphical interfaces, where each dialogue is a state and the events making you move between different dialogues are the buttons or menus you use.

Hardware, like tape recorders, traffic lights, CD players, microwave ovens and mobile telephones are other classic examples which are often found in books about digital technology, and the models are excellent as a basis for test design.

13.1 The Model
Here, we use what are called Mealy Graphs[62], where the state is represented by nodes and the links between the nodes represent transitions. The alternative is Moore Graphs, where the events are represented by nodes.[63] You can simply change the form of representation by changing each arc in the Mealy Graph to a node. We will do this later in this chapter in order to cover the graph with test cases. Mealy Graphs are simpler to work with since they:[64]:

1. More closely resemble what happens on their actual implementation
2. Have fewer states, and since;
3. The states are stable
4. You can repeat events more easily without the graph becoming more complex
5. It is easier to represent the graph in a table

We call the states *nodes*, and call connections between the nodes *links*.

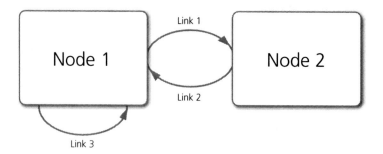

Figure 13.1: State Graphs consist of nodes and links. An arc is also called a transition. Links which start and end at the same node denote that an event does not lead to a transition, but it still undergoes some form of process.

The first step in compiling a graph is to describe the states an object can find itself in. The next step is to study which events can occur, and study, both the ones which make you move between states, and events which are to be overlooked by the system.

The most difficult but, at the same time, most entertaining part of the technique is compiling the model. The different sub processes included are:

1. Compile the different states an object can find itself in
2. Compile the transitions between the different states
3. Identify the events which cause a transition to occur
4. Define what happens during each transition

Since models are simplifications, there is seldom one single solution to each problem. It is always a balancing exercise, between having enough information to find all the interesting test cases, and not having so much detail that the model becomes unmanageable, and also usually invalid.

13.1.1 The ATM Machine

A good example is the classic Automatic Telling Machine or ATM. For teaching purposes, we will compile a very simplified graph for this. In reality, there are more states and events that are interesting to test and should be present in a complete graph.

1. The different states are as follows:
   a) Standby – nobody has inserted a card into the machine yet

b) Card inserted, request for PIN

c) PIN accepted – waiting for transaction

2. Draw arrows for the transitions according to the function descriptions

3. Events causing transition are:
   a) Insert card
   b) Enter correct PIN
   c) Enter incorrect PIN
   d) Enter correct transaction
   e) Enter incorrect transaction
   f) Choose to abort

4. What is carried out during transition is:
   a) Request new PIN
   b) Request new card
   c) Request transaction
   d) Eject money, card and receipt (execute transaction)

You have now created the picture below and the difficult work is complete.

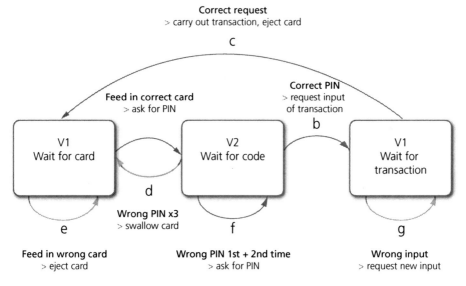

Figure 13.2: Very simple state graph for an ATM. In reality, there are more states and events that are interesting to test and should be present in a complete graph.

13.2 Creating Base Test Cases

13.2.1 Ways of Covering the Graph

There are a number of variants of how to fill in the graph you have drawn up, besides the one described above. Some of them are:[65] [66]

1. **Typical routes.** The most credible combinations
2. **The travelling salesman's route.** All different states in one test case.
3. **The Chinese Postman's route.** All transitions in the same test case, if there is that possibility.[67]
4. **Risk-based.** Routes where you think that a particular combination of transitions can cause problems.
5. **All routes a certain length.** From shortest to longest until you have covered all combinations. This is suited to automation, since it repeats many combinations and takes a long time to carry out.
6. **All ways of leaving a state.** For example, via a menu, function key, hot key, button and so on.
7. **All events which *should not* produce a transition.** Verifies the system's robustness.

13.2.2 Coverage According to Chow

One method is to cover, firstly, all transitions, then all transitions pairs, triples etc. This was originally presented by Chow.[68]

When you generate the test cases, there are different levels in the degree of coverage. Covering every individual transition is often called *Chow's 0-switch coverage*. This can be visualised in a simple table.

No.	Start	Event	Answer	End
a	V1	Right card	ask for PIN	V2
b	V2	Correct PIN	ask for transaction	V3
c	V3	Correct input	dispense money and card	V1
d	V2	Wrong PIN third time	swallow card	V1
e	V1	Wrong card	eject	V1
f	V2	Wrong PIN	ask for PIN	V2
g	V3	Wrong input	ask for transaction	V3

Figure 13.3: Table of the different transitions in the state graph for the ATM. The simplest form of test coverage is to test all the rows in the table.

13.2.3 Creating Test Cases

The next step is to generate the test cases and, in parallel with this, mark off the transitions you are covering.

Test Case 1
1. Insert card (V1)
2. Enter wrong code (V2)
3. Enter correct code (V2)
4. Enter transaction (V3)
5. Take card and money (V1)

Test Case 2
1. Insert wrong card (V1)
2. Take ejected card (V2)

Test Case 3
1. Insert card (V1)
2. Enter wrong code (V2)
3. Enter wrong code (V2)
4. Enter wrong code (V2)
5. Card is swallowed and you are back at the starting point (V1)

If we look in the table, we can establish that transitions 2, 3, 5 and 7 are covered in the first test case, transition 1 in the second and, finally, transition 4 in Test Case 3.

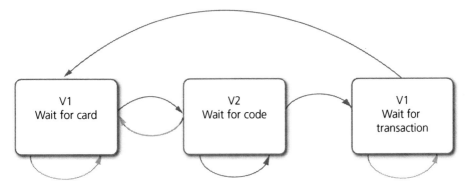

Figure 13.4: Graphic presentation of the transitions covered by Test Case 1. The lowest form of coverage is to test each transition at least once.

13.2.4 Transition Pairs

In order to achieve better coverage, you can use what we call transition pairs, involving two transitions in a row. The idea is that the result of an event in the system depends on what has happened in the preceding event. Sometimes, you will see the term 1-switch coverage.

13.2.4.1 Expanding the Table by one Column

There are two different ways of solving this, the first being to start with the first table and adding one additional column.

Analysis of our ATM produces the following 16 links:

V1	In	c	d	e
	Out	e	a	
	Produces the following arcs	15: c - e	9: d - e	2: e - e
		16: c - a	10: d - a	1: e - a
V2	In	a	f	
	Out	b	d	f
	Produces the following arcs	5: a - b	8: f - b	
		4: a - d	6: f - d	
		3: a - f	7: f - f	
V3	In	b	g	
	Out	c	g	
	Produces the following arcs	12: b - c	13: g - c	
		11: b - g	14: g - g	

Figure 13.5: Table showing development of transition pairs for the state graph ATM. We obtain all pairs by combining all routes into a node with all routes out of it. Even self-transactions, where we stay on the same node after transition, are counted.

The consolidated table is below, but columns showing event/answer have been taken out in order to simplify the table – this is already described in the first table, which describes the transitions.

No.	Start	Next	End
1	V1	V1	V2
2	V1	V1	V1
3	V1	V2	V2
4	V1	V2	V1
5	V1	V2	V3
6	V2	V2	V1
7	V2	V2	V2
8	V2	V2	V3
9	V2	V1	V1
10	V2	V1	V2
11	V2	V3	V3
12	V2	V3	V1
13	V3	V3	V1
14	V3	V3	V3
15	V3	V1	V1
16	V3	V1	V2

Figure 13.6: Consolidated table of transition pairs for ATM state graph. A more accurate form of coverage is to test all combinations of two transitions. Obviously, this requires more test cases.

If we look in this table of transition pairs, for Test Case 1, we manage to cover transition pairs 3, 8 and 12. As expected, more test cases are thus required in order to cover all transition pairs.

13.2.4.2 Creating a Dual Graph

You can also generate a dual graph, where the transitions represented earlier by links are substituted by nodes: in other words, a Moore graph. This way of testing all paired transitions is called the de Bruijn algorithm.[69] To generate a dual graph, you do the following::

1. Generate a graph where the links in the original have been changed to nodes.

2. Everywhere in the original graph where arc 1 comes into a node, and arc 2 goes out of it, draw an arc between node 1 and node 2. Every arc will now represent a transition pair.
3. Cover all links now with test cases.

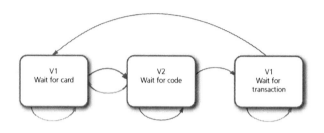

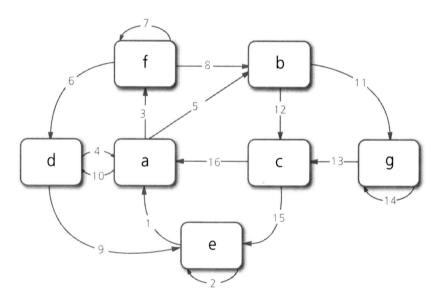

Figure 13.7: Original and dual graph for the ATM. An alternative to developing the table of transition pairs is to create a Moore graph, where each transition represents a transition pair in the Mealy graph.

ESSENTIAL SOFTWARE TEST DESIGN

13.2.5 Transition Triples and More

You can proceed to more stringent requirements by setting up transition triples and quadruples, by adding another column in the table of transition pairs. The problem is that the number of test cases grows very quickly, so it is often difficult to test all of the pairs without automating the tests. It is common to use at least transition pairs and, if you find many defects, to press on, with more advanced tests in certain areas.

13.3 Test Data

We can identify the following test data and combine this with test cases at the same time:

		TF1		TF2	TF2
Parameter	Group	a	b	a	b
Card	Valid card	X	X		
	Invalid type ICA, IKEA, OK			X	
	Restricted card				X
PIN number	Valid	X	X		
	Invalid once	X	X		
	Invalid twice				
	Invalid three times				
Balance	< 100 SEK				
	100 - 2000 SEK	X			
	> 2000 SEK		X		
Withdrawal	Defective input				
	100 - 2000	X			
	≥ 2000				
	100		X		
	2000				
	Same as balance				

Figure 13.8: Table of test cases and test data for the ATM. How you can combine different values in test cases are shown here.

13.4 Advanced Testing

To achieve a more advanced form of testing, you can use the list below for inspiration:

- Give the graph more detail
- Parallel users
- Ways of aborting the system lying outside the user's control
- Automated tests based on the graph: long-term tests for robustness

13.5 Example: the Windows Clock

Harry Robinsson is one of the leading experts in model-based testing. His aim is to automate his tests by creating formal models of objects he is testing.[70] The benefit of this type of more formal, model-based testing is that it is adaptable to the rapid changes always taking place. Thereby we also avoid what is known as the *Pesticide Paradox*, which involves the system becoming resistant to our test cases, meaning that we no longer detect any new defects. We are also involved early on, and can detect defects in the design. Since we are using automation, we can run large numbers of test cases which also test robustness.

Example: the Clock in the old versions of Windows

Here is a model of parts of the application clock.exe present in earlier versions of MS Windows, but not in Windows XP.

The clock is started by double-clicking on the file clock.exe, or choosing the clock from the menu.

It can be shown in analogue or digital form – change occurs through a selection from the Settings menu

It can also be minimised and restored by using the icons in the window.

Figure 13.9: Clock.exe is available both with and without frame and menu. This is counted as two different states. Source: Harry Robinsson (2005): EuroSTAR Presentation.

The figure below shows parts of the complete model. Since *About* is only an information window, I have chosen to describe it as a state, regardless of where you are coming from. What remains is the following:

1. The function Maximise produces a parallel picture of the model above, which sits together with it. The model in total is thus double the size.

2. The variables GMT, Seconds and Date, Select All to see or not see, with details. We should be able to create new states for all these parameters, but the problem is that the model grows extremely quickly – if we were to choose all these parameters as different states, the model's size would double for each parameter. The alternative is to define these parts as parameter within each state.

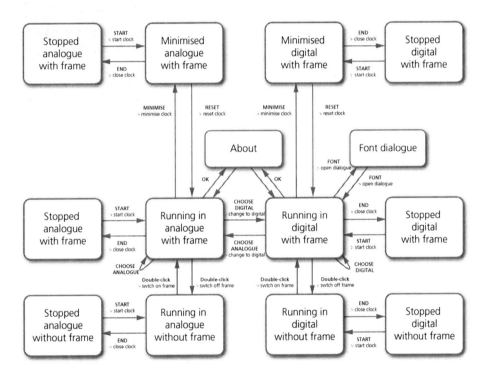

Figure 13.10: Part of the state graph for the Clock. The function Maximise produces a parallel picture of the model above, which sits together with it. The model in total is thus double the size.

From above, we get the following test data

Parameter	Group
Seconds	On
	Off
Date	On
	Off
Show GMT	On
	Off

Figure 13.11: Table of test data for the Clock. In this case, the test data are very simple.

Example of test case:
Test case 1: Start analogue clock, maximise, close, start, minimise, start, zero(?) stopwatch etc. Only the flow is tested here: we are not concerned with the data yet. The clock shrinks with each sequence.

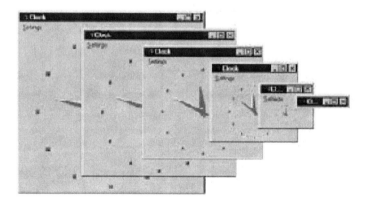

Figure 13.12: The Shrinking Clock. The effect of repeated sequences.[71]. Source: Harry Robinsson (2005): EuroSTAR Presentation.

ESSENTIAL SOFTWARE TEST DESIGN

Test case 2: We also deal with data: the Sequence *Start-minimise-stop-start-zero-date*: Result: The year disappears

Figure 13.13: The Disappearing Year. Lost year setting, which occurs after a certain sequence of transitions.[72] *. Source: Harry Robinsson (2005): EuroSTAR Presentation.*

13.6 Example: Pension Insurance

Here, we present a variation used in parallel with the planning of tests on a system for the administration of pension insurance. Central to the system is its handling of each insurance policy over its lifetime within the system, from when it is created, to when it finishes. The graph describes status as state, and change in states as links between the states. Dotted lines mean that the transition is not tested.

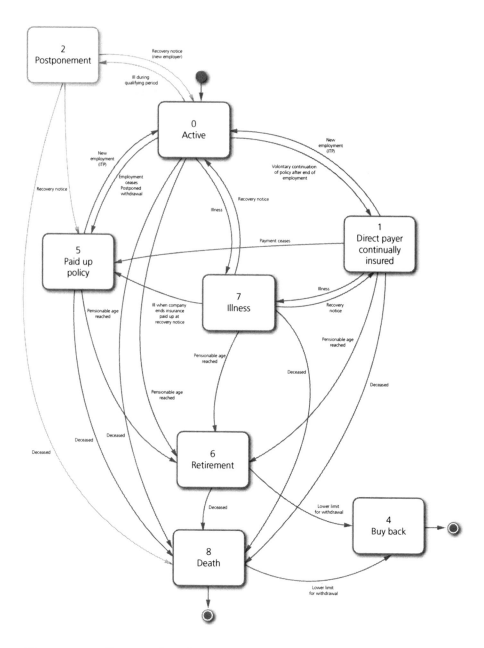

Figure 13.14: *State machine for pension insurance. Central to the system is its handling of each insurance policy over its lifetime within the system, from when it is created, to when it finishes.*

ESSENTIAL SOFTWARE TEST DESIGN

To perform risk-based testing, we chose to prioritise the tests based on statistics on present states and the most recent occurring change. The figures are written in here on the graph.

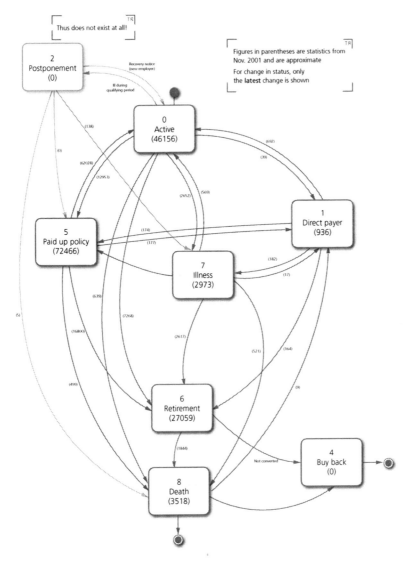

Figure 13.15: State machine with statistics on the number of insurance policies per status recorded in each state, and the most recent change recorded on the links.

The simplest form of test coverage (0-switch coverage) has been written into the picture. To obtain details about coverage of a higher degree (1-switch and 2-switch), a table should be used.

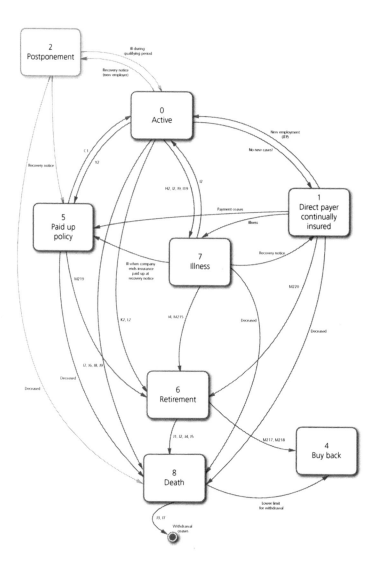

Figure 13.16: State machine with the test cases recorded on the links. In this case, all transitions are covered, but not all pairs.

ESSENTIAL SOFTWARE TEST DESIGN

13.7   Exercise 1 – Alcohol Lock

13.7.1 Use case – Alcohol Lock

Summary Description

The driver gets into the car to start it. Before the car can be started, the driver has to blow into the alcohol lock. As soon as the engine turns off, the driver has to blow again to be able to start the car.

Main Flow
1. The driver sits in the driver's seat and blows into the alcohol lock.
2. The car measures the alcohol content in the exhaled air.
3. If the amount of alcohol is below the boundary value, a green lamp lights up on the instrument panel.
4. The driver turns the key in the ignition in the car within 15 seconds after an approved measurement.
5. The engine starts
6. The driver turns of the ignition again
7. The engine stops

Alternative Flows

Below are all the alternative flows for the use case.

A1 – The amount of alcohol exceeds the boundary value

In point 3 in the Main flow, this happens when the amount of alcohol exceeds the boundary value:

1. A red lamp lights up on the instrument panel. The alcohol lock triggers, meaning that the car cannot be started for one hour.
2. After one hour, the lock releases and the driver can blow again.

A2 – More than 15 seconds elapse between the breath test and the car being started

To prevent a change of drivers after blowing into the alcohol lock, a maximum of 15 seconds may elapse between the breath test and starting the car.

In point 4 in the Main flow, more than 15 seconds elapse from the lamp lighting up to the driver starting the car. This then happens:

1. The alcohol lock reverts to standby status. Information about the failed ignition is saved. The driver may start again at point 1 in the Main flow if he/she wants to start the car.

A3 – The driver does not blow hard enough

In point 1, if the driver does not blow hard enough, so no measurement is registered, this happens:

1. The use case is complete. The driver may start again at point 1 in the Main flow if he/she wants to start the car.

A4 – Second time in a row that more than 15 seconds elapse between breath test and ignition

To prevent a change of drivers after blowing into the alcohol lock, a maximum of 15 seconds may elapse between the breath test and starting the car.

In point 4 of the Main flow, more than 15 seconds elapse from the lamp lighting up and the driver starting the car, this being the second time in a row that this happens. This then happens:

1. A red lamp lights up on the instrument panel. The alcohol lock triggers, meaning that the car cannot be started for one hour.
2. After one hour, the lock releases and the driver can blow again. End of use case.

13.7.2 Assignment
1. Compile the different states
2. Compile the transitions between the different states
3. Identify the events which cause a transition to occur
4. Define what happens during each transition
5. Draw up a table containing the above information
6. Generate two test cases from the above information, and mark off which variations they cover.

13.8   Exercise 2 – Tape Recorder

In this case, we have a tape recorder with the buttons PAUSE, PLAY, STOP, REW, FFW.

The logic is the following:
1. The PAUSE button places the tape recorder in standby mode and can be used in all given situations, regardless of whether the tape is running or not: pressing PAUSE again ends this standby mode.
2. To switch between the modes PLAY, REW and FFW, you have to go via the STOP button.

Assignment

1. Compile the different states the tape recorder can find itself in
2. Compile the transitions between the different states
3. Identify the events which cause a transition to occur
4. Define what happens during each transition
5. Generate test cases from the above information

FOOTNOTES

[62] Mealy G.H. [1955] *A Method for Synthesizing Sequential Circuits»* Bell *System Technical Journal* 34 pp. 1045–1079

[63] Moore E.F. *«Gedanken Experiments on Sequential Machines In Automata Studies, Annals of Mathematical Studies* No. *34 Princeton, NJ: Princeton University Press*

[64] Beizer, Boris[1995], *Black Box Testing* pp. 210–211

[65] Kaner, Cem, Jack Falk, Hung Nguyen[1999]: *Testing Computer Software*

[66] Robinsson Harry, Steven Rosaria [1999]: *Applying Models in your Testing Process, Intelligent Search Test Group, Microsoft Corporation*

[67] Kwan, M-K. [1962] *«Graphic Programming Using Odd and Even Points», Chinese Journal of Mathematics, Vol. 1*

[68] Chow, T.S. [1978] *«Testing Software Design Modeled by Finite-State Machines», IEEE Transactions on Software Engineering 4*

[69] Gross, J. and Yellen, J. [1998]: *Graph Theory and its Applications*

[70] Robinsson Harry, Steven Rosaria [1999]: *Applying Models in your Testing Process, Intelligent Search Test Group, Microsoft Corporation*

[71] Robinson, Harry: [2005]: *EuroSTAR Tutorial*: Presented with the author's permission.

[72] Robinson, Harry: [2005]: *EuroSTAR Tutorial*: Presented with the author's permission.

14 DECISION TABLES AND DECISION TREES

TO ANALYSE AND test complicated sets of rules, where several variables are used, you can use a technique called decision tables. The object is to analyse the rules in existence, both to find out whether the set of rules is logically correct, and to identify suitable test cases.

14.1 The Model
The technique involves listing the variables included in the set of rules, and the different combinations of the variables at hand. An example of how the template for a decision table may look is shown below. Sometimes the rules involved are written vertically in columns and, sometimes, horizontally in rows. The top row contains a number of logical rules here numbered 1 to 4. Each condition tests the combinations which are marked in the column below.[73] A figure one in the field means that the condition is true, a zero that it is false. This form of decision table where there are binary values only is called a truth table. The result can be marked with a cross or written out in plain text. This way, you get a general picture of all the combinations at hand. From the table, you can then compile appropriate test cases.

	Rule 1	Rule 2	Rule 3	Rule 4	...
Condition 1	0	1	0	1	
Condition 2	0	0	1	1	
Condition 3	0	0	0	1	
...					
...					
Result 1	X				
Result 2		X	X	X	
...					

Figure 14.1: Table of a format example for a decision table. The top row contains a number of logical rules numbered 1 to 4. Each condition tests the combinations marked in the column below. You can use X or 1, or write the value directly into the table.

Another variant of a decision table that I often use, with good results, is to write the rules as rows. [74] At the same time, this makes it simple to generate a file in which each test case is a row, which is in the same format as most files sent between systems. It is also easier to read than the earlier table, which consists mostly of ones and zeros.

Rules	Age	Gender	Type of car	Additional charge	Excess total
1	≤ 25	Male	Family, mid - range	1500	2000
2	≤ 25	Male	Sports	2500	3000
3	≤ 25	Female	Family, mid - range	0	500
4	≤ 25	Female	Sports	1000	1500

Figure 14.2: Part of a decision table for a set of rules. If every rule is written as a row, it is simple to generate a file in which each test case is a row, which is in the same format as most files sent between systems.

It can be difficult to know whether the table is correct just by reading through it. In order to quality assure the set of rules, you can transfer the same information to a tree structure, which is much easier to review. For a set of rules which is all-encompassing, and not overlapping, it is feasible to compile decision trees in order to describe the different combinations at hand in graphic form. You can then compile the test cases, either from the table, the tree, or both in combination. Compiling tables and trees is an effective form of quality control for the requirements.

A system or a large set of rules cannot usually be described in a single table, but has to be divided up into smaller parts. This can best be done in such a way that each part is independent of the others, otherwise you have to keep an eye on all the dependencies yourself. Always check that all the tables cover all the rules between them, and also that they do not overlap!

Example: We have a system which handles personal item insurance, where you can insure your car. We choose to compile test cases for the function which calculates the excess on the policy by creating a decision table and a decision tree.

ESSENTIAL SOFTWARE TEST DESIGN

14.1.1 Identifying Parameters and Groups

From the function to be tested, we firstly compile all the different parameters included in the set of rules. Any parameters that *do not* have any effect should also be left out. Split up the value set for each parameter into groups according to the rules at hand. In this case, «business rules» are for calculating the personal risk:

- Business Rule 1: As a starting point, the excess for all policy holders is 500 kronor
- Business Rule 2: Men under 25 years of age are subject to an excess increased by 1500 kronor
- Business Rule 3: Everyone over 25 with a «family» type care are subject to an excess reduced by 200 kronor
- Business Rule 4: All persons between 45 and 65 are subject to an excess reduced by 100 kronor, regardless of other discounts
- Business Rule 5: «Sports» cars attract an excess increased by 1000 kronor, regardless of other parameters
- Business Rule 6: «Mid-Range» cars do not affect the excess
- Business Rule 7: Everyone over 65 surrenders all discounts

From this, we compile parameters and groups:

Parameter	Groups
Age	≤ 25
	$> 25, \leq 45$
	$> 45, \leq 65$
	> 65
Gender	Male
	Female
Type of car	Family
	Sports
	Mid - range

Figure 14.3: Grouping of variables for the business rules. From the seven business rules, we split up the parameters involved into appropriate groups.

14.1.2 Summarising the Rules in a Table

Generate a table, say, in Excel. Each parameter has its own column, and each row symbolises a combination of decisions and, therefore, one leaf on your tree: we call them rules but they must not be confused with the business rules above. Empty field means that the value does not matter.

Rules	Age	Gender	Type of car	Additional charge	Excess total
1	≤ 25	Male	Family, mid - range	1500	2000
2	≤ 25	Male	Sports	2500	3000
3	≤ 25	Female	Family, mid - range	0	500
4	≤ 25	Female	Sports	1000	1500
5	> 25, ≤ 45	*	Family	- 200	300
6	> 25, ≤ 45	*	Sports	1000	1500
7	> 25, ≤ 45	*	Mid - range	0	500
8	> 45, ≤ 65	*	Family	- 300	200
9	> 45, ≤ 65	*	Sports	900	1400
10	> 45, ≤ 65	*	Mid - range	- 100	400
11	> 65	*	Sports	1000	1500

Figure 14.4: Decision table on the excess rules. Each parameter has its own column and each row symbolises a combination of decisions and, therefore, one leaf on your tree.

As soon as we generate the table, we discover that Business Rules 3 and 7 contradict each other. After discussion with the requirement assessors, we get an updated Business Rule 3:

2: **Everyone between 25 and 65 years of age** with a «family» type car attracts an excess reduced by 200 kronor

14.1.3 Quality Assuring the Table by Creating a Decision Tree

To check that the set of rules above is correct, we use a method called a decision tree. Begin with parameters that all rules on the same branch utilise. Then, continue in turn with the parameter which most rules utilise in order to prevent the same rule being split between several branches. For example, you should not use the gender parameter for people over 25 years of age – since this will double the number of leaves.

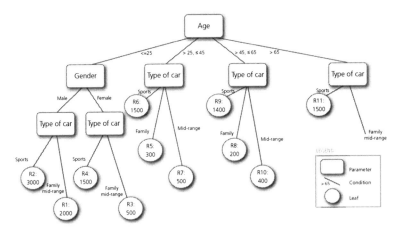

Figure 14.5: Decision tree for our insurance policy excess model. By drawing up a tree on this format, we are checking that the set of rules is logically correct. We can see that the branch furthest on the right has no leaves for the family and mid-range classes of car, which means that something is missing.

We find out whether several leaves overlap each other, or whether one branch is not complete. We can see that the branch furthest on the right has no leaves for the family and mid-range classes of cars, which shows that our set of rules is invalid, or that we have drawn up our table incorrectly. We decide that it was our table which was missing a row, and therefore add Rule 12.

Rules	Age	Gender	Type of car	Additional charge	Excess total
1	≤ 25	Male	Family, mid - range	1500	2000
2	≤ 25	Male	Sports	2500	3000
3	≤ 25	Female	Family, mid - range	0	500
4	≤ 25	Female	Sports	1000	1500
5	> 25, ≤ 45	*	Family	- 200	300
6	> 25, ≤ 45	*	Sports	1000	1500
7	> 25, ≤ 45	*	Mid - range	0	500
8	> 45, ≤ 65	*	Family	- 300	200
9	> 45, ≤ 65	*	Sports	900	1400
10	> 45, ≤ 65	*	Mid - range	- 100	400
11	> 65	*	Sports	1000	1500
12	> 65	*	Family, mid - range	0	500

Figure 14.6: Supplemented decision table for policy excess. We supplement a new row in order to achieve a complete table. The set of business rules has not changed.

Now, we have a complete set of rules in the table and supplement the graph with the last rule.

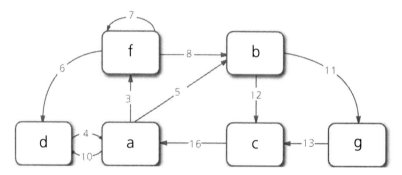

Figure 14.7: Updated decision tree for our excess model. Supplemented with the last leaf.

14.2 Creating Base Test Cases

Each leaf on the tree becomes a base test case. The tree will look different, depending on which order you chose variables. However, this should not affect how good the test case turns out to be. You can, if you want, develop test cases directly from the table above and ignore the tree, but the main reason why we compile the tree structure is to check that our set of rules is correct.

What we have not taken into account in this situation are the different invalid cases which can exist. If it is possible, one way or another, to put in values other than those that are valid, we must have some kind of error handling function. This issue ought to be taken up with those setting the requirements, and developers, in order not to risk losing sight of it. I prefer to have error handling functions separate from the set of rules by running a check on the data before we start to work with it.

TIP: When you run test cases, you can easily use the tree to identify where any defects have arisen. Start from the leaf where the test case has come to rest, and the leaf you expected it to come to rest on, and follow the branches upwards until their flows cross each other. You will find the defect in the condition where the flows meet.

14.3 Test Data

In this case, we already have a complete table with the different groups. If we add the boundary values, we have the complete test data table.

Parameter	Groups
Age	0
	> 18? Additional test values?
	≤ 25
	25
	> 25, ≤ 45
	45
	> 45, ≤ 65
	65
	> 65
	120 (maximum)
Gender	Male
	Female
Type of car	Family
	Sports
	Mid - range

Figure 14.8: Table of test data for the excess function. Step three in the test design process involves compiling groups of test data.

For every test case, i.e. every leaf, you choose one or more compilations of test data. How many test cases you need to have depends on how the logic in the program looks. You do not necessarily need to test boundary values or invalid values for each base test case. Partly, there is often an external error handling function which prevents invalid values from creeping through into the set of rules, for example *«if there are errors in the input data, send a message to the user or move the actual message to the error handling list»*.

14.4 Exercise: Decision Table for Field Controls in a Dialogue Picture

Examples from actual projects are always interesting. I have picked out a dialogue picture from the bank, where new accounts are created, names and terms are verified, but the structure of the set of rules corresponds to the original. The description of which fields are on the page contains a set of rules describing which fields have to be filled in. The task here is to compile a decision table for the rules, and to consider which test cases are appropriate for each rule. On the other hand, it will not suffice in this case to generate a decision tree. Why?

Field name / Button	Controls/Functions
Name on card	Name on customer's card. Mandatory, read - only
Customer number	Customer's number. Mandatory, read - only
Fi - group	Shows which Fi - group the instruction applies to. For Fi - group 01 Clearing mode must be filled in
Clearing mode	Here the valid clearing modes are given to create Euro clearing messages. These are for present KASS, CEDE and EUCL. Clearing mode must be filled in if Fi - group 01 is filled in.
Instrument class	Must be Eurobond or blank. Is given is the customer has a special account for Eurobonds. If instrument class is filled in, all fields above must be filled in.
Business type	The business types can be AVM, BSP, DEP, EMU and DFO. Is given if the customer has different ECL accounts for different types of business. If business type is filled in, all fields above must be filled in, apart from instrument class, which can be blank.
Country	The country code is given here. Country, in combination with currency, can be a criterion for different accounts. With different currencies in the same country, e.g, if the customer uses DKK and EUR in Denmark. If country is given, all fields above must be filled in, apart from instrument class, which can be blank.
Currency	Gives the business' payment currency. If currency is given, all fields above must be filled in, apart from instrument class, which can be blank.
Account	Customer's account for the registered combination. Must always be filled in. Euroclear, Kasseverein account or Cedel account

Figure 14.9: Description of parameters in the dialogue picture. How do we test the check on the input values?

14.5 Exercise: Decision Tree for a Complicated Set of Rules

Here is another example from an actual project. This also comes from the world of banking, where the set of rules is used to determine the creditworthiness of a borrower. The test object is only one fifth of the original, total and more complicated set of rules. The names of the parameters and values are fictional, but otherwise correspond to the structure of the set of rules.

Each rule initially looks like this:

Rule 1: If the person owns property, and has no official non-payment notice, and had a capital loss in the preceding year no greater than 100,000, this rule applies and the person gets a rating figure of 3.

To make the problem manageable, the table below was generated. Empty squares mean that we are not concerned about what value is written there. Remember that no rules should overlap each other, and that the rules must cover all types of people. Compile decision trees and test cases for the table below. Is the set of rules right?

One tip is to deal with half of the set of rules at a time, first, rules 9–20, then rules 1–8, and finally, to put them together in a shared tree. See the chapter about domain tests for a walkthrough of some of the ambiguities.

Rule	Owns Property	Age	Liability order	Capital loss previous year	Income previous year	Income/age	Income before tax	Has own company	Increase in income from previous year
1	Yes		No	≤ 100					
2	Yes	≤ 42	No	> 100	≤ 120				
3	Yes	≤ 42	No	> 100, ≤ 426	> 120	≤ 50			
4	Yes	≤ 42	No	> 100	> 120	> 75			
5	Yes	> 42	No	> 100					
6	Yes	≤ 42	No	> 100, ≥ 426	> 120	> 50, ≤ 75			
7	Yes	≤ 42	No	> 426	> 120	≤ 75			
8	Yes		Yes						
9	No	≥ 55					> 1000		
10	No	≥ 55					≤1000		
11	No	> 25, < 55	No	≤ 5	≤ 120			No	
12	No	> 25, < 55	No	> 5, ≤ 25	≤ 120			No	
13	No	> 25, < 55	No		> 120				
14	No	> 25, < 55	No	> 25	≤ 120			No	
16	No	> 25, < 55	No		≤ 120			Yes	
17	No	> 25, < 55	Yes						
18	No	≤ 25							> 1.2
Default				NULL	NULL		NULL		
				(or)	(or)		(or)		

Figure 14.10: Table of complicated sets of rules. From this table, you have to draw up a tree in order to see whether the set of rules is complete and not overlapping.

FOOTNOTES

[73] Pol, Martin, Ruud Teunissen, Erik van Veenendaal [2002] Software Testing – A Guide to the TMAP Approach pp. 223–236

[74] Binder, Robert[2000]: Testing Object-Oriented Systems

15 ELEMENTARY COMPARISON

ELEMENTARY COMPARISONS ARE a structural technique which is often used to cover flows for program logic in component tests. However, it is also excellently suited to later test levels. [75] [76] It requires knowledge of the function you are to test. We use something called Boolean algebra in order to describe the rules, and then develop appropriate test cases out of the total set at hand.

Complex functions require a whole lot of work in order to be sufficiently tested. Even small functions with only a few conditions require a very large number of test cases, if you are to perform comprehensive testing. For the most part, it is impossible to cover all variants. You have to make do with a fraction of the possible test cases. For functions with many different variables, it is especially important to have a structure procedure for achieving good coverage with a limited number of test cases. Here is a description of one technique called elementary comparisons.

A function can consist of a number of rules – in turn, these can consist of single or combined conditions. The technique starts with the following simplification of the original problem:

1. each condition/parameter involved must determine the result once
2. All the different results must be achieved at least once.

15.1 Boolean Algebra and Matrices

We call a rule that has only one condition «simple». For simple rules, there are two alternatives: either the condition is true, or it is false. This can be written in a truth table with each condition as its own column, where o means false, and 1 true. The column furthest to the right is the result of the rule, where the value is equal to the columns to the left. A rule consisting of many conditions in combination is called a compound rule. A rule with two conditions, where one of them must be true for the rule to be true, looks like this, $A \vee B$ read as A or B:

$$
\begin{vmatrix} 0 & 0 \\ 0 & 1 \\ 1 & 0 \\ 1 & 1 \end{vmatrix} = \begin{vmatrix} 0 \\ 1 \\ 1 \\ 1 \end{vmatrix}
$$

Figure 15.1: The compound condition (A or B). The truth table shows that, if one of the variables is true, the result of the condition is therefore true.

For this rule, all three conditions must be true for the result to be true. The formula $A \wedge B \wedge C$ is read as A and B and C. It can be written as:

$$\begin{vmatrix} 0 & 0 & 0 \\ 0 & 0 & 1 \\ 0 & 1 & 0 \\ 0 & 1 & 1 \\ 1 & 0 & 0 \\ 1 & 0 & 1 \\ 1 & 1 & 0 \\ 1 & 1 & 1 \end{vmatrix} = \begin{vmatrix} 0 \\ 0 \\ 0 \\ 0 \\ 0 \\ 0 \\ 0 \\ 1 \end{vmatrix}$$

Figure 15.2: The compound condition (A and B and C). The truth table shows that the result is true only if all variables are true at the same time.

We notice that the number of variations rises exponentially, as 2n. For a rule with six conditions, the number of variations is two to the power of six, which is 64. In a very short time, there are too many variations to test. Elementary comparisons build on making a smart choice of a smaller number of test cases, and still achieving good coverage through all parameters being tested in their own right, and all different results being achieved some time.

15.2 The Model

Example: The function for calculating the cost of membership of a tennis club has the following set of business rules:
- R1: If you are 18 years or under, membership is free (Age)
- R1: For people over 18 years of age, the basic charge is 2000 kronor
- R2: If the person is older than 40 years, has a monthly income of less than 20,000 kronor, and has no official non-payment notices against them, they get a discount of 500 kronor (R2) (Age, salary and non-payment notice)
- R3: If the membership type is «gold» or their playing level is «elite», an extra charge of 500 kronor is added (R3) (membership type and level)

Describe the conditions
We number the rules R1 to R3. Rows one and two are merged into one rule where the one applies in all situations where the other does not.

ESSENTIAL SOFTWARE TEST DESIGN

Rule 1 is simple. If age is less than 18, the parameter is false and the result is false, i.e. membership fee is 0 kronor. If age is greater than 18 years, the parameter is true and the result is true, i.e. membership fee is 2000 kronor. This is written in the following way:

Rule	Age > 18	Result	Test condition
R1.1	0	0	Age up to 18 years
R1.2	1	1	Age over 18 years

Figure 15.3: Table for Rule 1. If age is less than 18, the parameter is false and the result is false, and vice versa.

For rule R2, we can see that there is a positive result only if all included variables are true. If we test the case in which all included values are correct, and then, in turn, test to see whether each included condition (age, salary and non-payment notice) is false, this should give us good coverage of the logical conditions. Thus, we quite consciously skip the cases in which several conditions are simultaneously false. In the table below, we therefore skip the first four rows.

Rule	Age > 40	Salary < 20000	No liability orders	Result	Test condition
	0	0	0	0	More params. simultaneously false
	0	0	1	0	
	0	1	0	0	
	1	0	0	0	
R2.1	0	1	1	0	Age determines that the result is false.
R2.2	1	0	1	0	Salary determines that the result is false.
R2.3	1	1	0	0	Liability order determines that the result is false.
R2.4	1	1	1	1	Result true

Figure 15.4: Table for rule 2. Here, we firstly let age determine the result of R2.1, by allowing the other variables to be true, while age is false. Finally, we bring in the variation where we have had a positive result in R2.4. This way, we end up with half as many test cases as there are possible combinations.

Here, we firstly let age determine the result of R2.1, by allowing the other variables to be true, while age is false. We do the same thing with the parameters salary and non-payment notice which, in R2.2 and R3.3, may determine the result. Finally, we bring in the variant where we have had a positive result in R2.4. This way, we end up with half as many test cases as there are possible combinations.

15.3 Creating Base Test Cases

Next, we put together a summary table with all the conditions involved, and combine them in a number of test cases. The aim is to cover all rows in the summary table. In Test Case 2, there is a connection between Rules 1 and 2, since the condition (age < 18) automatically means that the condition (age > 40) is false.

	Description	Test Case 1	Test Case 2	Test Case 3	Test Case 4
R1.1	Age ≥ 18	X		X	X
R1.2	Age < 18		X		
R2.1	Age > 40 is false, so the rule is false		X		
R2.2	Salary < 20k is false, so the rule is false.	X			
R2.3	Liability order = Yes, so the rule is false.			X	
R2.4	All conditions true, so the rule is true				X

Figure 15.5: Summary table for Rules 1 and 2. The summary table contains all included conditions. We combine them in a number of test cases. Remember that the Age parameter is present in both rules.

15.4 Test Data

The next step is to use equivalence partitioning and boundary value analysis in order to compile the appropriate test data for each rule involved.

15.4.1 Table of Data

Analyse the variables, and divide the value set up into equivalence partitions.

Parameter	Groups and boundary values	Comments/value
Age	0	New - born family member? Is there a minimum age?
	≤ 18	
	> 18, ≤ 40	
	> 40	
	18	Boundary value
	19	Boundary value
	40	Boundary value
	41	Boundary value
	120	If we can handle 120, we can also handle all other living members!
	Detail missing	Can we register a person without a personal identification number?
Salary	< 20 000	
	≥ 20 000	
	19999	Boundary value
	20000	Boundary value
	0	Boundary value
	Max?	999999999 (max field size)
	Detail missing	Is this the same thing as not giving a discount? Think about whether the member does not wish to reveal salary.
Liability order	Yes	
	No	
	Detail missing	Do we do a credit check? How often, then?

Figure 15.6: Table of test data for the rules. Groups and boundary values are developed for all variables involved.

15.4.2 Suggestion for Complete Test Cases

Test Case 1a: Let us say that member Peter Jonsson is 45 years old, has a salary of 45,000, and has no official non-payment notice. The expected result is a membership fee of 2000 kronor.

Test Case 2a: Member Nils Andersson, who is 15 years old, has a salary of 0 kr and has no official non-payment notice. The expected result is a membership fee of 0 kronor.

Test Case 3a: Member Pelle Svensson, 43, has a salary of 12000 kronor, but has official non-payment notice. The expected result is a membership fee of 2000 kronor.

Test Case 4a: Member Nils Andersson, 41, has a salary of 19999 kronor and has no official non-payment notice. The expected result is a membership fee of 1500 kronor after discounts.

15.5 Advanced Testing

In this case, we can imagine a club with many different members who, together, cover all the different combinations we wish to test. Then, we experiment by administering the club's membership over at least one year end. Here are some test ideas as an appropriate start:

- Change the parameters so that the members' fees are changed.
- It is especially interesting when a new date means that a Junior Member becomes a Senior Member etc. If people pay for the whole year, or between two different dates, how is the age calculated? Do you become a Senior on the same day, month or year that you turn 18?
- How often do we ask the Credit Information Centre about official non-payment notices?
- What applies to the membership fee: is it paid on a full-year basis, or from the day you join?
- Is there a period of notice to quit? How should this be dealt with?
- Can we delete members or block them from future membership?

15.6 Exercise

1. Continue with rule R3 and build on the table.

> *(R3) If the type of membership is «gold» or their playing level is «elite», or ball subscription = Yes, or racket service = Yes, an extra charge of 500 kronor is added (membership type, level, ball subscription)*

2. Create test cases so that all conditions are covered: do you need to write more or can you supplement the ones already there?
3. The technique you have used, in this case, has removed some combinations of the variables. Is there any risk in this?

FOOTNOTES

[75] Pol, Martin, Ruud Teunissen, Erik van Veenendaal [2002] *Software Testing – A Guide to the TMAP Approach Elementary Comparison* pp. 237–245

[76] *The technique is also known by the name Modified Condition Decision Coverage (MCDC)*

16 COMBINATORIAL TESTING

THIS CHAPTER IS written by Mats Grindal and is published with the permission from the author. It is based on Mats´ doctoral thesis *Handling Combinatorial Explosion in Software Testing*

The aim of combinatorial testing is to provide a solution to combinatorial explosion[77]. In simple terms, combinatorial explosion occurs when a test problem can be described as a set of parameters each with a number of different values and the total number of possible combinations of parameter values is too big to be feasible.

To illustrate combinatorial explosion during test case selection, consider testing the «classical» function *triangle(side1, side2, side3)*. The three inputs represent the three sides of a triangle and the function returns a classification (equilateral, isosceles, scalene, or not valid) of the triangle. Any test case for the triangle function contains a combination of values of the three parameters. It is easy to see that the total number of combinations of parameter values is far too big to test exhaustively.

Combinatorial explosion during configuration identification occurs in a similar manner. Consider testing (a part of) a Web based system which should support several different operating systems (Windows, MacOS, Unix, Linux), different browsers (2 versions of Internet Explorer), and different types of data connections (modem, three ADSL speeds, and fiber optical connection).

The main purpose of combinatorial testing is to identify a manageable set of combinations. Combination strategies are algorithms that do this. All combination strategies require a description of the test problem in a model containing parameters with associated parameter values. Figure 16:1 contains a very simple model of the triangle testing problem for demonstration purposes. Invalid here can be missing value, non-integer, negative number etc. Each side of the triangle is represented in the model as a separate parameter. The input space of each parameter is divided into partitions containing one or more values. Each partition is referenced by its parameter name and its index. For instance, <A3> means that side1 of the triangle should contain a value that is equal to or higher than 10.

Index	1	2	3	4
Parameter A (side1)	0	1-9	10-	Invalid
Parameter B (side2)	0	1-9	10-	Invalid
Parameter C (side3)	0	1-9	10-	Invalid

Figure 16:1: Input parameter model of triangle example.

Based on the model, combination strategies select combinations of parameter values, for example <A1, B2, C3>, until some coverage criterion is satisfied.

16.1 Coverage

The ability to vary coverage is a central concept in combinatorial testing. Higher coverage will give you better test quality but also more test cases/configurations. Figure 16:2 shows a subsumption hierarchy of the most commonly used coverage criteria used in combinatorial testing. A coverage criterion X subsumes another coverage criterion Y if and only if 100% coverage with respect to X automatically results in 100 % coverage with respect to Y[78]. Subsumption is indicted in the figure by arrows.

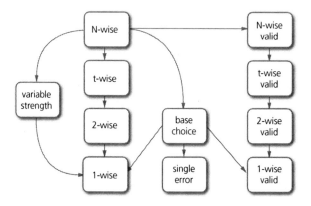

Figure 16:2: Subsumption hierarchy for combination strategy coverage criteria.

The simplest form of coverage used in combinatorial testing is *1-wise coverage*. It requires each parameter value of every parameter to be included in at least one combination. Figure 16:3 shows a set of combinations that satisfies 1-wise coverage with respect to the model of the triangle problem in Figure 16:1.

Id	Combination
1	A1, B1, C1
2	A2, B2, C2
3	A3, B3, C3
4	A4, B4, C4

Figure 16:3: 1-wise coverage of the triangle example.

ESSENTIAL SOFTWARE TEST DESIGN

A natural extension of 1-wise coverage is *2-wise* (pair-wise) coverage. It requires every subcombination of values of any two (pair) of parameters to be included in the set of combinations. Figure 16:4 shows a set of combinations that satisfies 2-wise coverage with respect to the model of the triangle problem in Figure 16:1.

Id	Combination	Id	Combination
1	A1, B1, C1	9	A3, B1, C3
2	A1, B2, C2	10	A3, B2, C4
3	A1, B3, C3	11	A3, B3, C1
4	A1, B4, C4	12	A3, B4, C2
5	A2, B1, C2	13	A4, B1, C4
6	A2, B2, C3	14	A4, B2, C1
7	A2, B3, C4	15	A4, B3, C2
8	A2, B4, C1	16	A4, B4, C3

Figure 16:4: 2-wise coverage of the triangle example.

A generalization of 1-wise and 2-wise is *t-wise coverage*, which requires every sub-combination of values of any t parameters to be included in the set of combinations. The highest possible coverage criterion with N parameters in the model is *N-wise coverage*, which in other words is the same as every possible combination. In our triangle example this would be $4*4*4=64$ test cases. It is also possible to have different levels of coverage for different parameters in the same model. This is called *variable strength coverage*.

Usually test cases containing more than one invalid value are less effective in detecting faults[79]. The main reason is that code for error handling generally checks the input values one at a time and as soon as the first invalid input value is found the error handler is invoked and the execution is terminated. Hence, if there is a fault related to the second invalid value, this fault may be masked by the first invalid value. The coverage criteria described so far (1-wise, 2-wise, t-wise, N-wise, and variable strength coverage) do not take the meaning of the parameter values into account. In other words, if any of these coverage criteria are used for test case selection, there are no guarantees that combinations will contain at the most one invalid value. See for instance combination 4 in Figure 16:3 and combinations 4, 13, and 16 in Figure 16:4.

To be able to take this observation into account we need to know for each parameter value in the model, whether it represents a valid or an invalid partition. Figure 16:5 shows the model from Figure 16:1 with this information added. Zero is considered valid input even though there can never be a triangle with one side that is zero in length. The reason is that «not a valid triangle» is a defined result.

The classification of the partitions into valid and invalid partitions can be used to define more coverage criteria.

Index	1	2	3	4
Parameter A (side1)	V: 0	V: 1-9	V: 10-	I: Invalid
Parameter B (side2)	V: 0	V: 1-9	V: 10-	I: Invalid
Parameter C (side3)	V: 0	V: 1-9	V: 10-	I: Invalid

Figure 16:5: input parameter model for triangle example with semantic (Invalid or Valid) information added.

The *t-wise valid coverage* criteria from the subsumption hierarchy in figure B require t-wise coverage of valid values across the parameters. Figure 16:6 shows a set of combinations that satisfy 2-wise valid coverage with respect to the model of the triangle problem in Figure 16:5. Note that none of the combinations Figure 16:6 contains any invalid value.

Id	Combination
1	A1, B1, C1
2	A1, B2, C2
3	A1, B3, C3
4	A2, B1, C2
5	A2, B2, C3
6	A2, B3, C1
7	A3, B1, C3
8	A3, B2, C1
9	A3, B3, C2

Figure 16:6: 2-wise valid coverage of the triangle example.

Single error coverage represents an opposite of t-wise valid coverage. To satisfy *single error coverage* each invalid parameter value has to be included in a combination where all the other parameter values are valid. Figure 16:7 shows a set of combinations that satisfy single error coverage with respect to the model of the triangle problem in Figure 16:5. It is possible to generalize single error coverage with respect to the number of invalid values included in a combination but this would give the exact results that Beizer says we should avoid.

Id	Combination
1	A4, B2, C3
2	A2, B4, C2
3	A2, B3, C4

Figure 16:7: Single error coverage of the triangle example.

The final coverage criterion included in the subsumption hierarchy in Figure 16:2 is called base choice coverage[80]. The first step to satisfy base choice coverage is to identify a base combination. The base combination consists of the base values of each parameter. The tester is free to pick any value as the base value but it is recommended to pick the valid value that is most often used. From the base combination new combinations are derived by altering the values of one parameter at a time such that each value of that parameter is included in at least one combination while keeping the rest of the parameters fixed in their base values. Figure 16:8 shows a set of combinations that satisfy base choice coverage with respect to the model of the triangle problem in Figure 16:5 under the assumption that the base combination is <A2, B2, C2>.

Id	Combination	Id	Combination
1	A2, B2, C2	9	A2, B3, C2
2	A1, B2, C2	10	A2, B4, C2
3	A3, B2, C2	11	A2, B2, C1
4	A4, B2, C2	12	A2, B2, C3
5	A2, B1, C2	13	A2, B2, C4

Figure 16:8: Base choice coverage of the triangle example.

Although all coverage criteria may be applied to any test problem, it is usually the case that invalid values are not included in the model when using combinatorial testing to identify configurations to be tested. This means that single-error coverage as well as the t-wise valid coverage criteria are usually not used in configuration testing.

Obviously every test problem is different so it is very difficult to give specific recommendations with respect to which coverage criterion that should be used but there exist some general observations which may be of help. It is generally the case that moving upwards in Figure 16:2 will give increasing numbers of combinations which means longer test times but better test quality. For small test problems the difference in size between different coverage criteria is generally small and for large test problems the opposite is true.

When using combination strategies for test case selection, 1-wise coverage usually gives too low test quality since there is no consideration of how values of different parameters are combined. Instead, base-choice, 2-wise, 2-wise valid and single error coverage are better choices.

When configuration identification is the topic, parameters usually do not contain invalid values. Further, each configuration takes some time to set-up and to test so time is often an important factor. For this reason, 1-wise and base choice coverage are often good choices.

Exercise:

1) Compute the amount of 2-wise coverage of the input parameter model in Figure 16:1 that is achieved by the sets of combinations given in, Figure 16:6 (2-wise valid coverage), and Figure 16:8 (base choice coverage).

16.2 Combination Strategies

Combination strategies are algorithms that select a set of combinations from an input parameter model, such that the selected set of combinations satisfy some coverage criterion. A goal with most combination strategies is to keep the set of combinations as small as possible. This goal is relatively easy to fulfill for simple coverage criteria, such as 1-wise, base choice, single error, and 1-wise valid. In fact, for all of these coverage criteria it is possible to find minimal sets of combinations. In contrast, for the more complex coverage criteria, such as 2-wise, 2-wise valid and higher, the problem of finding a minimal set of combinations that satisfy the coverage criterion is more difficult.

More than 20 combination strategies exist[81]. Some of the more known are *Each Choice*[82] (EC) that satisfies 1-wise coverage, *Base Choice*[83] (BC) that satisfies base choice coverage, *Automatic Efficient Test Generator*[84] (AETG) that satisfies t-wise coverage for t ≥ 2, and *Orthogonal Arrays*[85] (OA) and In *Parameter Order*[86] (IPO), both satisfying 2-wise coverage.

With the exception of OA, the other four combination strategies operate by step-wise extending a set of combinations until the identified combinations satisfy the coverage criterion. In each step, one or more candidate combinations are evaluated and the one that adds most coverage is picked. This common property makes all these combination strategies simple to automate, which is reflected in the forthcoming section on combination strategy tools.

Orthogonal Arrays differ from the rest of the combination strategies in that it is not based on a step-wise algorithm. Instead it is based on a combinatorial concept called Latin Square. A Latin Square is an N x N sized square filled with N types of elements such that each row and each column contain exactly one element of each type. A correctly solved Sudoku is an example of a 9x9 Latin Square with the elements {1–9}. Latin Squares can be used to derive a set of combinations that satisfy 2-wise coverage for a given input parameter model. In fact there are mathematical proofs that the set of combinations is minimal with respect to the number of combinations in the set. This and the fact that sets of combinations for test problems with varying sizes can be pre-calculated makes orthogonal arrays appealing. However, there are also some downsides. First, the identification of combinations it is very difficult to automate. This means that if no pre-calculated set of combinations exist for the current test problem it is a manual task to create one. Second, and perhaps more important, is restrictions in the sizes of test problems that orthogonal arrays can handle. For some test problem sizes orthogonal arrays cannot help. Third, the guarantee for a minimal set of combinations only works for test problems that are balanced, i.e., that it has exactly the same number of values for each parameter. Taken together these downsides probably makes orthogonal arrays less attractive than other combination strategies in the general case.

16.3 Input Parameter Modeling

One of the key success factors of combinatorial testing is input parameter modeling, i.e., deciding how to represent the test problem in an input parameter model. In most cases it is possible to define several different models for the same test problem. The contents of the model have a direct impact on the quality of the test cases. As an example, compare the two input parameter models of the triangle problem illustrated Figure 16:1 and Figure 16:9, respectively.

Index	1	2	3	4
Parameter A (input types)	Integers	Reals	Non-numbers	x
Parameter B (result)	Equilateral	Isosceles	Scalene	Not valid
Parameter C (longest side)	side1	side2	side3	x

Figure 16:9: Alternative input parameter model for the triangle problem.

It is clear that both models represent the triangle problem. It is also clear that the two models cover slightly different properties. The contents of the model have a direct impact on the quality of the test cases. The models in the example have been derived using two different approaches. The model in Figure 16:1 has been created with a structural approach to modeling, whereas the model in Figure 16:9 is based on a functional approach.

16.3.1 Structural Input Parameter Modeling

In structural input parameter modeling[87], the parameters in the interface of the test object are mapped one-to-one onto parameters in the input parameter model. The triangle example has three parameters, which means that the resulting input parameter model also has three parameters. The input space, i.e., the set of possible input values, of each parameter is then partitioned individually. The main advantage with the structured approach is that it is a simple task to create the input parameter model. The drawback with the structural approach is that there are no guarantees that the resulting test cases will take all aspects of the functionality of the test object into account. To see an example of this, consider the combination <A2, B2, C2> of Figure 16:1. This combination requires the tester to select values for the three sides of the triangle from the value domain {1–9}. This leaves the tester with several choices. If the same values are selected for all three sides the result is an equilateral triangle. If two sides are given the same values and the third side is smaller that the sum of the two other sides the result is an isosceles triangle. It is also possible to select values of the three sides of the triangle such that the result is scalene or not valid. The important observation is that the same combination may result in very different test cases and there is no guarantee that every important result will be covered in the final test suite.

16.3.2 Functional Input Parameter Modeling

In functional input parameter modeling[88] it is not necessary to consider each input parameter in isolation and we are not restricted to only include properties of the input parameters in the model. Instead we can model aspects of the functionality and possibly the state of the test object. For instance, parameter B of the model in Figure 16:9 represents the different results of the triangle classification and both parameters A and C affect all three input parameters. The major advantage with the functional approach is that it generally results in test cases with higher quality than test cases from a structural model. The two drawbacks are that it may be difficult to identify the input parameter model parameters and it may be difficult to translate a combination into actual inputs of the test case since the values of more than one parameter may affect the same input parameter.

Regardless of the modeling approach there is some general advice for creating input parameter models. (1) The model should be complete, which means that there should be enough parameters in the model to cover all interesting aspects of the test object. (2) Each parameter should also be complete. This means that every possible physical value should be represented by some value of that parameter. (3) There should be no overlap in the model. Overlap means that the same physical value is represented by more that one value of the same parameter.

As previously stated, combinatorial testing can be used to identify configurations to be tested. In this case, the input parameter model represents the different possible configurations. The task of creating an input parameter model for configurations is generally easier than creating an input parameter model for test case selection. The reasons are that a structured approach to modeling is usually a good idea, and that the model does not need to include invalid values for the different parameters.

16.4 Conflicts in the Input Parameter Model

Input parameter modeling sometimes result in models in which some of the sub-combinations are strange or even meaningless. As an example consider the model in Figure 16:9. The meaning of the sub-combination <A3, B1> is unclear. What does it mean to use non-numbers to create an equilateral triangle? Other sub-combinations, in the model in Figure 16:9, with unclear meanings are <A3, B2> and <A3, B3>. If A3 (non-numbers) are interpreted to hold for all three sides at the same time then it is also unclear how to combine A3 with any of the values of parameter C. Any impossible or semantically meaningless sub-combination is called a conflict.

There are three general ways of handling conflicts. These are (1) *designing the models without conflicts*, (2) *avoiding selection of combinations containing conflicts*, and (3) *replacing combinations containing conflicts* with other combinations such that the original coverage is preserved.

Designing the models without conflicts may result in lower test quality since conflicting values or even parameters may have to be omitted from the model. Omitting a value or parameter from the model, due to a conflict, means that this value cannot be combined with other values with defined meanings. For instance if value A3 is removed from the model in Figure 16:9, there can be no combination containing the sub-combination <A3, B4>, which is a combination with defined meaning. Designing the models without conflicts can also be achieved by splitting the original model containing conflicts into several conflict-free sub-models. Although this will preserve the original coverage, it will instead result in unnecessary large sets of combinations[89].

A better way both in terms of effectiveness (preserving coverage) and efficiency (keeping the set of combinations as small as possible) is to avoid the selection of combinations with conflicting sub-combinations. For this to work, this mechanism has to be built into the combination strategy. Although this may not be a problem in theory, it can be a practical problem since many tools come without access to the source code, which in this case is necessary if conflict handling is not already built into the tool.

The third way to handle conflicts is to replace conflicting combinations with other combinations such that the original coverage is preserved. To illustrate this, consider the combinations in the first column (labeled «Original») in Figure 16:10, which satisfy 2-wise coverage with respect to the model in Figure 16:9. For simplicity, we only consider the three conflicts [<A3, B1>, <A3, B2>, <A3, B3>].

Original		Clone		Replace	
Id	Combination	Id	Combination	Id	Combination
1	A1, B1, C1	1	A1, B1, C1	1	A1, B1, C1
2	A1, B2, C2	2	A1, B2, C2	2	A1, B2, C2
3	A1, B3, C3	3	A1, B3, C3	3	A1, B3, C3
4	A1, B4, C3	4	A1, B4, C3	4	A1, B4, C3
5	A2, B1, C2	5	A2, B1, C2	5	A2, B1, C2
6	A2, B2, C3	6	A2, B2, C3	6	A2, B2, C3
7	A2, B3, C2	7	A2, B3, C2	7	A2, B3, C2
8	A2, B4, C1	8	A2, B4, C1	8	A2, B4, C1
9	A3, B1, C3	9a	*, B1, C3	9a	A2, B1, C3
10	A3, B2, C1	9b	A3, *, C3	9b	A3, B4, C3
11	A3, B3, C1	10a	*, B2, C1	10a	A1, B2, C1
12	A3, B4, C2	10b	A3, *, C1	10b	A3, B4, C1
		11a	*, B3, C1	11a	A1, B3, C1
		11b	A3, *, C1	11b	A3, B4, C1
		12	A3, B4, C2	12	A3, B4, C2

Figure 16:10: The steps to replace conflicting combinations while preserving coverage. Conflicts marked in bold.

In the first step, the conflicting combinations are cloned. In each clone one of the conflicting values is replaced by an arbitrary non-conflicting value, represented by a wild card (*). In the second step, the wild cards are replaced by specific values such that no new conflicts are introduced. In this example, replacing the conflicting combinations results in three extra combinations compared to the original set of combinations. It is generally the case that the replace method will slightly increase the set of combinations but unless the number of conflicts is very large, this increase is usually insignificant.

16.5 Tools

One of the main strengths of combinations strategies is the relative simplicity to automate the combination selection. This has resulted in several commercial and free tool implementations. Good news is that there is a Web site dedicated to combinatorial testing[90], which contains, among other things links to more than 20 different tool suppliers.

When deciding on tools there are several properties to look for. (1) Which coverage criteria are supported by the tool. (2) To what extent can the tool handle conflicts in the input parameter model? (3) Does the tool support predefined combinations? (4) Can the tool export its results in any known format? (5) What infrastructure does the tool require? (6) What does the tool cost?

New tools are constantly added to the web site and existing tools are updated and improved so it is very difficult to state which of the tools that is best. However, a couple of tools are worth mentioning.

PICT[91] is a free Perl-based tool from Microsoft supporting t-wise coverage as well as 2-wise valid coverage, single error coverage, and variable strength coverage. It supports conflicts and pre-selection of test cases. Despite the rather crude user interface this is probably the most powerful tool at the moment.

Telcordia[92] offers a Web commercial, based service in which the user enters an input parameter model in a Web interface and a resulting set of combinations is returned to the user. This service is based on the AETG combination strategy, which means that there is support for t-wise testing for t≥2. There is also support for handling conflicts in the input parameter model.

FOOTNOTES

[77] Grindal, M. [2007]: *Handling Combinatorial Explosion in Software Testing*

[78] Rapps, S. and Weyuker, E.J. [1985]: *Selecting Software Test Data Using Dataflow Information*

[79] Beizer, B. [1990]: *Software Testing Techniques*

[80] Ammann, P. E. and Offutt, A. J. [1994]: *Using Formal Methods to Derive Test Frames in Category Partition Testing*

[81] Grindal, M. [2007]: *Handling Combinatorial Explosion in Software Testing*

[82] Ammann, P. E. and Offutt, A. J. [1994]: *Using Formal Methods to Derive Test Frames in Category Partition Testing*

[83] Ammann, P. E. and Offutt, A. J. [1994]: *Using Formal Methods to Derive Test Frames in Category Partition Testing*

[84] Cohen, D. M., Dalal, S. R., Kajla, A., and Patton, G. C. [1994]: *The Automatic Efficient Test Generator (AETG) system*

[85] Williams, A. W. and Probert, R. L. [1996]: *A Practical Strategy for Testing Pair-wise Coverage of Network Interfaces*

[86] Lei, Y. and Tai, K. C. [1998]: *In-Parameter-Order: A Test Generation Strategy for Pair-wise Testing*

[87] Grindal, M. [2007]: *Handling Combinatorial Explosion in Software Testing*

[88] Grindal, M. [2007]: *Handling Combinatorial Explosion in Software Testing*

[89] Grindal, M. [2007]: *Handling Combinatorial Explosion in Software Testing*

[90] *www.pairwise.org*, page visited in June 2007

[91] *http://download.microsoft.com/download/f/5/5/f55484df-8494-48fa-8dbd-8c6f76cco14b/pict33.msi*, page visited June 2007

[92] *http://aetgweb.argreenhouse.com/*, page visited June 2007

17 TESTING DATA CYCLES

MOST SYSTEMS HAVE a database supporting them. The different tables contain a whole range of logical objects, including a registered person, an account, an address, a purchase order and so on. What is common to most objects is that they have a life cycle, which means that, firstly, they are created, then changed and, finally, deleted or become inactive. The data cycle test involves a structured walkthrough of all functions which in some way change the objects.[93] This technique, which is intended for testing on a more overarching basis, focuses on step four in the process – advanced testing.

Referential integrity means that different objects are connected together, which implies that there are rules for how you can update them. For example, if you delete a customer from your register, the customer's address is deleted at the same time. Another example is that, for the same customer, you cannot have two different billing addresses where the ranges of dates for which they apply overlap each other. Check both that the objects are changed in the way you want, and that the reference integrity is preserved.

It is also a matter of checking that all objects are covered by CRUD, otherwise it is time to get hold of the requirements. If any part is missing, is it for a reason, or is something really missing.

17.1 The Model

Start by creating a table where all objects are written into a horizontal row. Beneath this, you list all the functions vertically in a column. The next step is to mark off in the table which objects are dealt with by which functions. The term CRUD stands for Create, Read, Update, Delete. If the table gets too big, it is a good thing to split it up into smaller parts.

Things to look for when doing this is what object should be allowed to be changed from what functions and what access rights do you need to modify or read a certain object. I have experienced the somewhat strange feature that when I want to add an attachment to an e-mail the system allows me to delete the files from their original place. I only expect to get read access from inside the attachment dialogue. Another problem is when you are allowed to update an object from several different dialogues that might do things slightly differently. That might really screw things up and is scornfully called spaghetti coding by the deveopers themselves.

	Object 1	Object 2	Object 3
Function 1	C	R	R
Function 2	R	R	C,U,D
Function 3	U,D		

Figure 17.1: Template for a simple CRUD-table for testing of data cycles. Each object has to be covered by all operations in CRUD – Create, Read, Update and Delete – if nothing else is explicitly stated.

17.2 Creating Base Test Cases for Each Object

Carry out the tests, so that you, firstly, create, then update and, finally, delete an object. As a check on whether this is working, you study the object by using the functions available for reading it between each update. Be careful to check that the reference integrity is preserved after each update. Note that you might have to have access to a database tool in order to check whether data is really removed or not.For each object, you have a number of test cases built up in the following way:

1. Create object, read object
2. Update object, read object
3. Delete object, (try to) read object

For example, for a bank account, it may look like this:
1. Create account, view account
2. Deposit to account, view account
3. Withdraw money from account, view account
4. Close account, (try to) view account

17.3 Test Data

You supplement with test data in the same way as for the other techniques, by analysing the relevant variable using the elementary techniques equivalence partitioning and boundary value analysis.

17.4 Determining the Order and Assumptions for the Test Cases

For the sake of flexibility, it is desirable to have as few assumptions as possible, since this causes dependencies between test cases, and governs how you can carry out tests. Most often, you cannot avert certain test cases from requiring other test cases to have been executed first. If, for example, you have to input a new billing address for a customer in a register, this requires the customer to exist in the first place, which means that the test case for this must be run first.

Create test chains and test packages for all test cases in your table. Next, compile the data needed so that the tests can be started.

17.5 Example: Variant of a CRUD Table

The table below is a variant which was used to plan the tests on a function which handles the repayment of amounts paid out to a customer. Our objects are job, operator, withdrawal and deposit.

No.	Function	Task	Person dealing	Withdrawal	Deposit
1a	Dialogue task	C,U	C		
1b	Batch task	C	C		
2	Accept task	U			
3	Batch for creating withdrawals	R,D*	R	C	
4	Dialogue dep/repay		R	R	C,U
5	Accept dep/repay			C, D*	R,U,D*

Figure 17.2: Example of a CRUD table for the testing of a function for handling customer refunds.

The work procedure is for the functions to be executed from the top down in the table. Here, it can also be interesting to check that only people with the right permissions may carry out the different operations.

1. A withdrawal task is created, usually, with the function *Batch Task (1b)* but can also be generated and changed via dialogue (1a).
2. The withdrawal is approved by an authorised operator via the dialogue *Approve Task*. In
3. Next, a batch program is executed, which processes all approved tasks. Parallel to this, a withdrawal is created. Also, the task is flagged as complete and, for legal reasons, this is saved in the database.
4. If the withdrawal fails, it comes back and has to be dealt with manually. The return is dealt with by a deposit of the same sum being created via the dialogue *deposit/return*

5. Finally, the deposit is approved by an authorised operator via the dialogue *Approve deposit/return*. The authorised operator can update data which is invalid. At approval, a new withdrawal is created, at the same time as the invalid one is deactivated (it is still in the system, but is inactive, and therefore flagged D*).

17.6 Exercise

1. Choose your most recent project or the system you administer.
2. List a pair, each of three different objects you can find, and the functions used to change or view them. Flag this in the table.
3. How were these tested the last time?
4. Suggest test cases
5. Compile appropriate test chains

FOOTNOTE

[93] Pol, Martin, Ruud Teunissen, Erik van Veenendaal [2002] *Software Testing – A Guide to the TMAP Approach Elementary Comparison* pp. 219–223

18 TESTING SYNTAX

SYNTAX IS ABOUT having one homogeneous format. The definitions of what syntax tests involve vary between different reference works. I have chosen to split up the concept into two parts: overarching and detailed. Overarching syntax tests involve detecting the incorrectly functioning format in the window, reports and other output data, and how the elementary controls on the input data for these are working. Forbidden values in different fields and windows should result in equivalent error handling. This is often part of the Usability tests. As a basis for this, you can use general standards, check-lists, data models and design documents. It is common for requirements, design and development of different parts to be dealt with by different people. These tests are a way of making sure we achieve a homogeneous application. Detailed syntax tests are performed on those areas where the format of a parameter is extremely carefully specified, for example, where it comes to handling dates, personal identification numbers or postal addresses.

18.1 Model – Overarching Syntax Tests
Start by creating a list of the windows and reports you want to test. For each object involved, you list the different fields and their format.

	Page header	Logo	Forename	Surname
Dialogue 1				
Dialogue 2				
Report 1				
Report 2				
Mailout 1				
Mailout 2				

Figure 18.1: Template for overarching syntax tests. It is important to have a homogeneous application, despite the fact that setting the requirements and the development have been carried out by different people.

18.2 Test Data – Overarching Syntax Tests
With the help of the field definitions and the elementary techniques equivalence partitioning and boundary value analysis, you compile appropriate test values.

It is especially important that all values are tested, so that long names and unusual symbols can be accommodated on all reports and outputs.

18.2.1 Check-listing Values

For the fields which are not subject to strict syntax control, you make appropriate use of the simple check-list below, with generic values for each field. In all likelihood, you have already tested correct normal values in the earlier test cases:

- Empty field
- Minimum number of characters/minimum value
- Maximum number of characters/maximum value
- Numerical characters
- Non-numerical characters
- Default values
- Invalid values
- A check that mandatory fields are filled in
- Format

There is nothing to say that you can enter invalid values in all fields, but you should try to type in invalid values into the fields where you can change the text yourself. You may need to perform a more accurate analysis of date fields and other fields that are just as strictly defined, since these require more checks than other fields.

18.2.2 Check-listing Layout

Use a check-list to check that:

- All elements are present – header, footer, logo, buttons, fields
- Titles, page header, page footer and buttons have the correct appearance and location
- Titles and information are consistent for all the windows and reports involved
- Function buttons work the same way across the whole application
- All parameters are shown in the same way in all elements

Example: syntax check-list

In this example, I registered myself via a form on the web as somebody interested in advertising bulletins about conferences on testing. The first two bulletins contained a couple of amusing and incorrect variations on the address label. The third bulletin consisted of a single card which had the address on an attached label, and the function appears to work correctly.

	Forename	Surname	Address	Country
Web registration	Torbjörn	Ryber	Värtavägen 73	Sweden
Letter 1	Torbj rn	Ryber	V rtav gen 73	Sweden
Letter 2	Torbj}rn	Ryber	V|rtav|gen 73	Sweden
Letter 3	Torbjörn	Ryber	Värtavägen 73	Sweden

Figure 18.2: Results from syntax tests where the format differs within the same system. Here, the different functions cannot handle Swedish characters.

18.3 Model – Detailed Syntax Checking

For the fields under strict syntax control, you need to perform more detailed tests. You describe what is applicable with a list of rules, which is successively broken down into its smallest components. One format which is common is the Backus-Naur Format – BNF (see below). All these rules must then be tested in detail: grouping of the test data are present already in the model.

Example: Swedish Personal Identification Number (Personnummer) according to BNF

Rule 1: Personnummer = Year Month Day «–» Number
Rule 2: Year = 1880 < Integer ≤ 2007
Rule 3: Month = 01 < Integer ≤12
Rule 4: Day = «01» < Integer ≤ «31» if Month = «01»| «03»| «05»| «07»| «08»| «10»| «12»
Rule 5: Day = «01» < Integer ≤ «30» if Month = «04»| «06»| «09»| «11»
Rule 6: Day = «01» < Integer ≤ «28» if Month = «02» if Year is not a leap year
Rule 7: Day = «01» < Integer ≤ «29» if Month = «02» if Year is a leap year
Rule 8: Number = N1 N2 N3 N4
Rule 9: N1, N2 = «0» < Integer ≤«9»
Rule 10: N3: «1»| «3»| «5»| «7»| «9» if the person is male
Rule 11: N3: «2»| «4»| «6»| «8»| «0» if the person is female
Rule 12: N4 = (control number calculated by a formula)

18.4   How Large is the Text?

A field in a report must be able to handle a particular number of characters. In the database, it does not matter which character it is, but actually how big is a written text string of 20 characters? There can be a big difference between upper and lower case characters, not the least depending on which character it is.

iiiiiiiiiiiiiiiiiii
WWWWWWWWWWWWWWWWWWWW

Are texts in different languages of different lengths? IBM estimates that a translation from English into other languages makes the space for the text increase by, for example:

English – number of characters	Other language – needs extra space
Max 10	101 - 200 %
11 - 20	81 - 100 %
21 - 30	61 - 100 %
31 - 50	41 - 60 %
51 - 70	31 - 40%
More than 70	30%

Figure 18.3: Translation from English to, for example, Swedish can require increased space for the text. Source: Cem Kaner et al. (1999):Testing Computer Software (Originally from IBM)

This can present problems, for instance, for menus and dialogues translated from English into another language. For example, take the *text Preview* which, in Swedish, becomes *Förhandsgranska*, which is twice as long.

19 TIME CYCLE TESTING

DIFFERENT THINGS HAPPEN in a system with a particular frequency. It can be a case of months, quarters, years or some other subdivision. Time cycles are often tested at higher levels, like system and acceptance testing. Examples of time dependent events are:

1. Sending out balance statements for bank accounts each month.
2. Sending out information for tax returns for all customers' accounts, including interest, tax and capital once a year.
3. Updating the bank's lending rate after rate rises – this happens regularly but not at fixed intervals.
4. Sending out welcome letters to all new customers joining yesterday, this week etc.

19.1 The Model

Find out what requirements there are for recurring events in the system. Sometimes, it is not written down, and then you have interview the business representatives.

This can give rise to a whole range of requirements on how long the test cycles must be and which test dates you must use. Often, you have neither the time, nor the opportunity to run tests over several years, but you organise the execution of tests in such a way that you still cover the points in time you want. A four-month test cycle beginning in December covers a change of year, four changes of month and a change of quarter.

This technique, which is intended for testing on a more overarching basis, focuses on step four in the process – advanced testing. Think about time cycles when you are carrying out the overarching execution plan, and filling in dates on the test schedule!

20 EXPERIENCE-BASED TESTING

PROBLEMS WITH QUALITY can be defined as the difference between what a person expects, and what arises in practice. With this definition as a starting point, risk can be defined as the likelihood that a quality issue will occur, multiplied by its effect. This is no precise formula, but at least it provides information about how great the risks are relative to each other. In principle, all testing is risk-based, so here, we focus mostly on how we can identify and rank the risks.

The aim is to identify what risks there are and, from the potential damage (the risk), build test cases. The final aim is both to detect and correct the problems which can arise, and also to build confidence in the system by establishing which risks do not arise.

Paul Gerrard describes risk-based test handling as having a number of risks at the start and, as testing proceeds, the risks disappearing one at a time. At every given moment in time, you know which risks have been tested, and which remain. This means that you, as test manager, can inform the project manager which parts of the system are working, and which remain to be tested. From this, decisions can be made about release, production and distribution for sale.[94]

Preferably, the requirements should be prioritised. This is often not what happens, which means that we testers have to ask questions of those placing the order and the project manager. However, it is not only the requirements which are the basis for how we handle risk: work method, technical solution and resources also have a role to play.

Error guessing is described as a situation where a person is good at detecting defects, helped by intuition and experience, and without using any specific technique.[95] The idea behind error guessing is knowing where defects tend to crop up. This is really nothing magical. Instead, the person performing the testing builds their assumptions on earlier experience or detailed knowledge about how a piece of software works. This chapter is precisely about correct testing on the basis of lists of known defects and weaknesses.

Below is a number of different approaches which all have their different strengths, with some being more technical, some more general. The degree of formality also varies. Terms vary from experience-based testing and risk catalogues, to attack patterns, but the basic ideas are the same, namely of identifying possible defect risks from some kind of experienced-based list, and creating test cases for these.

20.1 Classic Risk Handling
One model used exceedingly often is the *classic* risk handling model which

builds on the fact that every project team conducts a risk seminar. Often, some form of generic risk lists are used, both for the project and the final product. The rest of this chapter deals with a number of procedures which all build on risk lists of some kind.

The result of the risk seminar is a list of risks which are determined by likelihood and effect. It is common to have three levels, marked one to three, or High, Medium and Low. If the likelihood and effect factors are multiplied together, we end up with a relative risk list, where the greatest risks are highest up.

Risk ID	Description	Likelihood	Effect	Risk factors
1	Technical solution not previously implemented can lead to an increase in time needed	1	1	1
2	Key resource Java booked in other projects	2	2	4
3	The requirements in the payments area is undergoing change	3	3	9

Figure 20.1: Classic risk list resulting from a risk seminar. The risks of the project can affect testing due to the fact that we have to spend more time on weaker elements.

Here, we have listed three different risks. The top one has a very high risk factor, since both likelihood and the effect associated with the risk occurring are high. The last risk, associated with the requirements being changed in one area, is low, since the likelihood that it will occur is low, and the effect will be little if it does happen. In principle, we can say that elements with the highest risk are tested early on, and with extra accuracy, while elements with low risk, or no risk at all, are tested later and less thoroughly. A new technical solution can lead us, not only to taking delivery of the code too late, but can also lead to the code containing more defects than usual. If vital resources are not available, it often means that another, less competent, person has been allowed to take over, which results in lower quality delivered to us for testing.

20.2 Heuristic Risk-Based Testing

James Bach describes risk-based testing as:

1. Making a prioritised list of risks according to a free choice method.
2. Testing in order to research each risk.
3. After risks disappear and new ones appear, adapting the tests so that they work to the actual risk list.

He describes one method which he calls heuristic risk-based testing. The technique is presented as check-lists of open questions or suggestions. You can attack the problem from within, by basing your questions on the technical design, or from outside, by considering what you want from the system.[96]

20.2.1 The Risks from Within
Here are a number of questions you can ask the developers, based on a graphical description:

- What happens if this component does not work?
- Can it turn out that this function is being carried out at the wrong time?
- What kind of error handling do you carry out here?
- What does this arrow mean?
- What external components is this process dependent on?
- How do you test this when you integrate it with the other elements?
- What are you most worried about?
- What do you think I should test especially carefully?

If you are cooperating well with the developers in this way, it provides you with a lot of information for your risk assessment. However, it does require you to have your own particular technical knowledge and experience in order to progress.

20.2.2 The Risks from Without
Look at the system from the point of view of what you want it to achieve. Here, you make use of three different lists of risks:

Quality Criteria
The following areas can be used to identify risks with the non-functional requirements. (Inspired by quality standard ISO-9126)

- Capability: Can the function be executed fully for all variations of data?
- Reliability: will the function work well and handle different problem scenarios?

- Usability: how easy is it for the average user to use the application?
- Performance characteristics: how does the application respond to your usage?
- Installability: how easy can the application be installed on your intended platform?
- Compatibility: how well does the application work with external components?
- Supportability: how economical is it to support users of the application?
- Testability: how easy is it to test?
- Manageability: how easy and expensive is it to manage and improve?
- Portability: can the application be moved to another platform?
- Localisation: how simple is it to publish the application in another language?

Generic Risk list

In all systems, there are generic risks. Here is a list of a number of common situations where you can count on the risk of defects occurring being higher than usual:

- Complex: large module, advanced connections, complex calculations.
- New: everything which is new.
- Changed: everything which has changed from last time.
- Functions which, if they go wrong, affect several other parts of the system.
- Functions dependent on many other parts of the system.
- Critical functions which, if they do not work, can lead to extensive damage.
- Functions which have to meet the requirements extremely precisely in order to be approved.
- Functions which will be used very often.
- Strategic parts which make this system much better than what the competition offers.
- Third-party solutions, where external agents have manufactured elements outside our direct control.
- Elements scattered in time of manufacture, or location in the system, but which have to work together.
- Parts known for having had many earlier defects.
- Elements in which you have just found defects.[97]

20.3 Risk Catalogues
There are a large number of risk catalogues on the internet, and in different

books. The book *Testing Computer Software* deals with a large number of lists based on different situations, like user interfaces, control flows or state graphs. Here is an extract from a risk list: [98]

User interface
- Functionality
- Communication
  - Information is missing
  - Instructions on the on-line screen are missing
  - Assumes that a written manual is available
  - Undocumented functions
  - States that appear impossible to exit
  - No cursor
  - The program does not show that it has deleted your input
  - No information about long waiting times, e.g. hour glass
  - Incorrect information
  - and so on

20.4 Attack-Patterns

James Whittaker has written two books [99] [100] about what he calls *Attack-Patterns*. James has a background as a developer and uses an approach for testing which keeps him close to the program. He starts by counting four different types of user:
- *Human*
- *File system*
- *Operating system*
- *External software*

He then categorises the software's functionality into four areas:
- *Input data handling*
- *Output data handling*
- *Data storage*
- *Calculations*

From these categories, a number of attacks are suggested for detecting conceivable defects. The aim and execution of each attack is described in detail.

The principle behind the approach is to deal with one problem at a time, and research it carefully from a technical perspective. The aim is to check elements lying outside the actual of each program, like, for example, error handling, initiation of variables and updates, and is similar to what we usually call *robustness tests*.

For testing how the user interface (human user) handles input data and output data, the following ten attacks are suggested:

- Use input data so that all the different error messages occur.
- Make sure that each function uses the default values available.
- Use all available value sets and data types.
- Place far too many sets of data in all fields.
- Test all combinations of variables which can be thought to work together.
- Repeat the same input data or sequences several times.
- Force out different output data for each set of input data.
- Try to force out invalid output data.
- Change the content in the output data you have obtained.
- Force the screen to update itself.

20.5 Taxonomies

Taxonomies are a way of classifying things on the basis of some characteristic they have as regards a specific purpose. Carl von Linné is often called the father of Taxonomy, since he classified plants in his *Systema Naturae*.

In testing, we can structure all the areas where a particular function or a particular aspect of a system can experience problems. From this, we obtain material for those test cases we have to develop in order to check for possible weaknesses: you can look upon this as a list of ideas we can use for inspiration. For example, you can see this book and its contents as a way of classifying techniques according to the types of defect usually found in software.

A very well written description of taxonomies, and a detailed example about web commerce, is *Shopping Cart Taxonomy* which is downloadable from the Internet, 236 pages, free of charge.[101]

20.6 Q-patterns

To end this chapter on risk-based techniques, I will deal with *Q-patterns* or *Question-patterns*, as Vipul Kochar calls them. Q-patterns are an attempt to formalise lists of questions in the same way as was performed for software design. They can also be an aid to formulating questions, for example, for the review of a design, or as a list of requirements for the purchase of login components from a third-party supplier, or for in-house development. Below is an extract from his presentation material.[102]

What are Q-patterns?

Q-patterns are a compilation of related questions grouped together. These questions relate to some part of the requirements on the software, and try to give you a number of alternatives which can be used to compile a solution. For your needs, you can either compile a solution directly based on the questions, or based on these requirements, create your own questions or test cases. You start with a good range of ready-made and ready-thought-out review comments, design strategies and test cases.

You can add things to existing Q-patterns or generate new ones according to need.

The aim is to compile a generic template which can be used for all types of pattern, and gather together all patterns for general access on the web. There is no such database developed at the time of writing, and the template is in MS Word format.

Example of Q-pattern for handling passwords

Password handling

Passwords are used for security, in principle, everywhere, but the implementation of them is probably not always the same. The same company may have different solutions in two different products.

NAME
Password handling

PURPOSE
The commonest way to authenticate a system or a user is to ask for a password. Password control can be found at different levels like users and groups, or different stages like operating system, application etc.

QUESTIONS
If you use password control anywhere in your application, you can ask the following questions:

Administration
1. Can the administrator reset the password?
2. Can the administrator's own password be reset?

3. What happens if the administrator forgets his or her password (default or reinstallation)?
4. Can the administrator determine the default password?
5. Can another administrator reset the administrator's password?
6. Can an administrator read a user's password?

Usage
1. What are the minimum and maximum lengths for the password?
2. Can we include numerals?
3. Can the password be blank?
4. Where is the password saved?
5. Is there a default password?
6. Can the default value be changed?
7. Can special characters like &, @, . or # be included?
8. How is a password changed: is the old password required?
9. Is there a message about confirming change of password?
10. If there is a «remember password» feature so that you do not have to write in the password every time you log in, is there supposed to be one?

User interface
1. Is the input of the password shown as * when you log in and change password?
2. How many * are shown? The same number as the number of letters not recommended?

Security
1. How are passwords saved? Are they encrypted, and which algorithm is used?
2. Is the password case sensitive?
3. Can the password be copied and pasted in?
4. Can an older password be reused and, if so, within which period of time, and with how many changes?
5. If there is a best-before date, what happens if the user does not log in until that date, if the user does not change password?
6. Is the number of failed login attempts counted in order to block login access after three attempts, or is there a similar feature?
7. Are logs kept of everything, even logins?
8. If logs are saved, are the passwords encrypted?

Performance characteristics

1. Do passwords consist of single or multiple changes?
2. How much time does authentication take at login?
3. How much space is needed to save passwords?
4. For an incorrect password, how much time does it take to generate a error message?
5. How many users can be authenticated at the same time?

Example: Q-pattern for password handling

This example is extremely simple. When we are working with complex patterns, and creating a library of cooperating patterns, the concept can take on greater relevance and become more useful to us.

FOOTNOTES

[94] Gerrard, Paul[2002]: *Risk-Based Test Reporting, StickyMinds.com*

[95] Myers, Glenford [1979] *The Art of Software Testing*, p.73

[96] Bach, James [1999]: *Heuristic Risk-Based Testing, Software Testing and Quality Engineering Magazine*, 11/99

[97] Appendix A in *Testing Computer Software*. (Kaner: Appendix A pp. 363–436)

[98] Kaner, Cem, Jack Falk, Hung Nguyen[1999]: *Testing Computer Software* pp. 376–377

[99] Whittaker, James: *How to Break Software*

[100] Whittaker, James: *How to Break Software Security*

[101] Giri Vijayaraghavan & Cem Kaner, *Software Testing, Analysis & Review Conference (STAR East), Orlando, FL, May 12–16, 2003. (Received the Best Paper Award at STAR), www.testingeducation.org/a/tecrf.pdf*

[102] Vipul was voted by the delegates to receive *LogicaCMG's Star-Award for the most original contribution* to the 2005 EuroSTAR Conference.

21 FOR THE DEVELOPER

THE MAJORITY OF techniques described in this book are also suitable for component tests. In short, many of the principles are the same, but the level of detail is different. This section deals with the elementary ideas of component testing. What is dealt with is important to know, but for it to be complete requires specific knowledge about the precise language you are developing in.

The benefit of testing an individual model on its own is that we achieve better control over the tests. This is necessary for making sure, for example, that all the code is covered. Problems in component testing are partly dependent on which programming language is being used, and often requires some form of tool so that it can be carried out. There are several books for developers who want to improve in testing in object-oriented programming [103] [104].

Important parts which should be part of a component test include:

- All error results
- Format controls
- Help texts
- Program logic compared to specification
- Data flow: correct handling of variables
- Control of code coverage

Two of the more central parts of component testing are *control flow* (*program logic*) and *data flow*[105]. These parts are described in a little more depth.

21.1 Testing the Program Logic

The first thing you do is to draw up a graph of the flow, in the same way as with, for example, use cases. The next step is to cover the different flow combinations in place. For the control flow, there are different ways of measuring the tests' degree of coverage, the commonest being listed below:

- Statement Coverage: All instructions executed at least once
- *Branch coverage* All *code loops* or *branches* have been walked through, which is to say that all results of all conditions have been tested
- Path Coverage: All *combinations of code loops* or *routes* have been covered. In principle, this is impossible to carry out except for very simple programs.
- *Elementary Comparison*: All conditions have been tested separately and all *results achieved* (*also called Modified Condition Decision Coverage.*)

The formula can be written as a flow. Here is a simple example for illustrating different degrees of coverage:

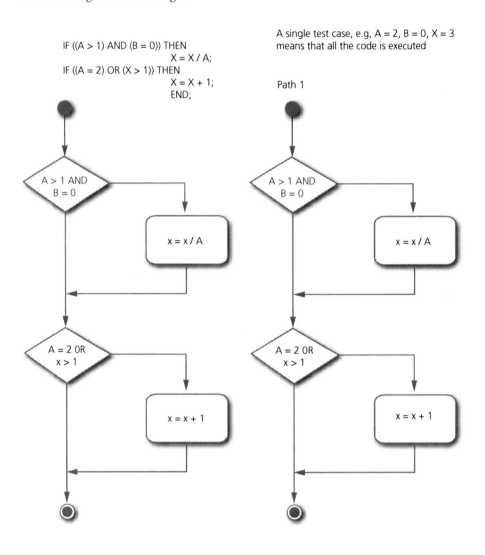

IF ((A > 1) AND (B = 0)) THEN
    X = X / A;
IF ((A = 2) OR (X > 1)) THEN
    X = X + 1;
END;

A single test case, e.g, A = 2, B = 0, X = 3 means that all the code is executed

Path 1

Figure 21.1: Formula and program flow for a simple program consisting of two conditions.

Figure 21.2: By running a single test case, all rows of code are covered. (Statement Coverage)

ESSENTIAL SOFTWARE TEST DESIGN

Another test case, e.g, A = 1, B = 1, X = 0 means that all the branches are executed. This is better, but is it enough?

Path 2

Covering all paths is reckoned by some to be the best form of coverage, which is wrong!

Path 3, Path 4

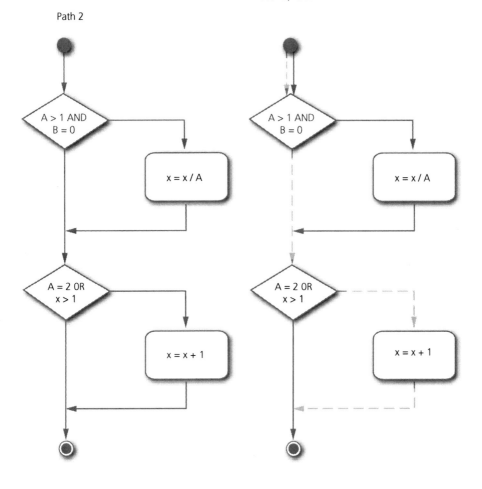

Figure 21.3: By running two test cases, you can cover all branches, which is significantly better. (Branch Coverage)

Figure 21.4: By running another two test cases, all parts are covered, which is the most complete coverage of the flow. (Path Coverage)

The four test cases required to achieve full coverage of all routes are listed in the table below. Despite the fact that we have achieved such good coverage, which happens to be impossible to attain in most cases, we still miss several defects. Coverage of different flows detects defects dependent on defects in the flows, but often misses partial conditions and variables that are involved.

Path	A	B	X	Problem
1	2	0	3	Misses the defect A > 1 OR B = 0
2	1	1	0	Misses the defect A = 2 OR X < 1
3	3	0	1	
4	2	0	5	

Figure 21.5: List of test cases giving full coverage of all routes. Misses the potential defects listed on the right.

A better type of coverage in this case is elementary comparisons. This involves all partial conditions being capable of determining the result some time, and all results of the condition having to be achieved, i.e. coverage of all branches. This type of coverage is called *Elementary Comparisons* or *MCDC* and have been discussed earlier in Chapter 15. With the help of this technique, we detect the two defects we missed in the previous example, when we were focusing only on covering the program flow.

A	B	X	Comments
2	0	3	First condition true
			Second condition true: A determines
0	0	0	First condition false: A determines
			Second condition false
4	1	2	First condition false: B determines
			Second condition true: X determines

Figure 21.6: Test cases for the elementary comparisons technique. With this technique, we achieve better (?) tests with fewer test cases.

ESSENTIAL SOFTWARE TEST DESIGN

This is supplemented with the elementary techniques *equivalence partitioning* and *boundary value analysis* in order to compile data so that invalid, extreme and boundary values are included. Despite the fact that only coverage of the program flow is an imperfect way of testing, coverage of all routes is said to be the most comprehensive form of testing program code, which the example above clearly shows is not the case.

21.2 Testing Data Flows

Different programming languages handle variables in different ways. In Java, variables are defined and used within a function between the brace parentheses { and } and disappear automatically when the function is over. In other languages, like C++, the variables must be declared explicitly, the writing area allocated and also cleared out when you are finished with them. Many more modern programming languages have compilers which solve most of these problems, in which case the example below solves itself automatically. I will not go into any further detail on the benefits and drawbacks of different languages.

In short, there are four things we can do with a variable: *define it*, *give it a value*, *use it* in some kind of formula and *delete it*.

Example:
- Define the variable Amount: defined as numerical, integer, 10 characters
- Assign a value. Amount = 123 678
- Use in a condition about Amount > 400 000
- Delete the variable

For describing which events are valid or invalid, we use a state graph with an associated table.

From	Event	To	Comments
Undefined	Define	Variable defined	OK
Undefined	Assign value	?	Not allowed
Undefined	Use	?	Not allowed
Undefined	Delete	?	Not allowed
Defined	Define	Define	Probable error of thought
Defined	Assign value	Variable has value	OK
Defined	Use	?	Not allowed
Defined	Delete	Undefined	Probable error of thought
Variable has value	Define	Defined	Probable error of thought
Variable has value	Assign value	Variable has value	OK
Variable has value	Use	Variable has value	OK
Variable has value	Delete	Undefined	OK

Figure 21.7: Tabular description of transitions of state for a variable. Permissible and forbidden operations on the variable.

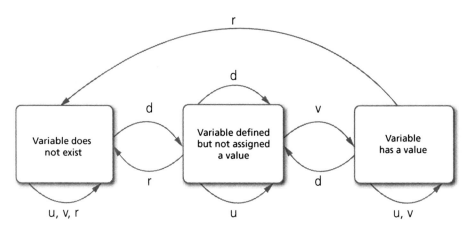

d: define | v: assign value | u: use | r: remove

Figure 21.8: State machine for possible events for a specific variable.

From the program flow you have compiled, you take one variable at a time and find out how it is used. You get either valid, invalid (incorrect) or strange events which probably depend on some kind of error in the thought process.

Example:
- From a route through the control flow, we find that the variable Amount is defined twice in a row without being used. Here, we may suspect that we have thought it through wrongly.
- Further on, there is a condition which says «if Amount > 400, then...», but Amount does not appear to have been assigned any value in the code preceding the comparison. This is a slightly more serious defect.

It is also important to remember which functions are permitted to do what, with which variables. It begins to look like a *CRUD analysis* – see the earlier chapter about testing *data cycles*. So, an important part of the tests is where the integrity of the data are handled correctly: the right data being changed by the right function in the right way.

21.3 Using Tools
For the practical execution of component tests, it is important to have a good tool. There are plenty of free variants on the web. Some of the commonest which are completely free are collected together under the concept XUnit. Examples are NUnit for C# and .Net or JUnit for Java. Commercial programs for program testers include JavaTest, for Java, and MFE, for Cobol. There is a multitude of resources on the web. It is just a matter of looking.

FOOTNOTES
[103] Binder, Robert[2000]: *Testing Object-Oriented Systems*
[104] McGregor, John, David Sykes[2001]: *A Practical Guide to Testing Object-Oriented Software*
[105] Copeland, Lee [2003]: *A Practitioner's Guide to Software Test Design*

PART III

PART III OF the book deals with practical details about how to organise your test cases, what you should think about when you are carrying out tests, and suggestions for handling defects.

22 ORGANISING THE TEST CASES

THIS CHAPTER CONTAINS practical details for how you can build and organise test cases. There are many different ways of doing this, and I have chosen here to present a set-up which has worked well for me in a good number of projects. Aside from developing the test cases, we must also link them up in an appropriate way so that the result is executable. To help us, we have things like test chains, test packages and execution plans.

The important thing for all test cases, is that they have the task of verifying one or more aspects of a system. The execution often begins with free-standing simple test cases for a limited area, which are not mutually dependent. These can be run in parallel, without an internal order. A test chain can be seen as a red line linking up several test cases which have to be run in series. Test packages, in turn, are a practical categorisation, where you put into the same package all the test cases which, for some reason, need to be carried out simultaneously. The execution plan links everything up in a detailed schedule. The picture below illustrates how it fits together.

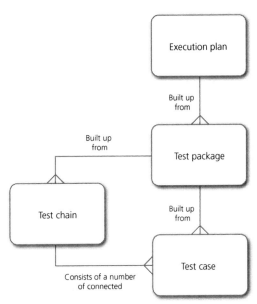

Figure 22.1: Picture of how you can organise your test cases. There is no absolute truth about how best to organise your tests: like everything else, it depends on the situation.

22.1 Test Cases

The description of a test case may differ in how it looks, depending on which test level at which it is found. For test cases at a higher level, it can be a good idea to use a template. The method described here works well for system and acceptance tests, where the test case involves the user integrating with the system.

There is a widespread perception that a test case should be so detailed that anybody can run it. This way of thinking has its drawbacks: it is not feasible to write down everything which is important, neither do I believe that just anyone can do a good job of carrying out tests. In most cases, it is better to write down less in detail, for two important reasons. Firstly, it takes far too much time to write down all the details and, secondly, changes always occur during the course of the project, so the likelihood of the details you write down being correct at the end of the process is very small.

It is important that a person familiar with the nature of the operation involved takes part in the test work, when it comes both to design and execution. This person does not need to be an expert in testing and, thereby, more or at least different information might be required in the description of the test case.

There is absolutely nothing to say that all test cases should be documented in this way. If you have to test, say, a batch function, and each test case consists of a row in a file, it is most likely inappropriate to force information into the template described below.

22.1.1 Size and Subdivision in Test Cases

Let practical considerations rule the day. The maximum size should suit about as long a period as you can manage to concentrate, or sit still in one session. Do not write test cases that are too large: that way, they take too much time, both to review and run.

If many actors are involved, it may be appropriate to divide the test cases up according to who will be carrying them out.

Example: *An operator creates a job for a customer who has missed a payment or payments on their mortgage. The job is then approved by an office manager and, depending on the size of the debt, there is another approval stage which rests with a regional manager.*

In this case, it is most practical to have three test cases, one for each actor involved.

You should remember that the test case has a clear purpose: when the purpose is achieved, the test case is finished. It is most often practical to have several different verification stages in each test case. However, if you have far too many steps in the same test case, you run the risk of it never successfully finishing it. There is no universal solution. Use experience, common sense and instinct!

22.1.2 Components
Administrative Fields
For handling the test cases, there are a number of administrative fields. The most important is the unique identifier. Write down an ID followed by a short description for clarity's sake. If you are using a document template, name the document after the designation. Think about how you assign names, for future sorting purposes. What other fields you use depends on what is most practical. Common fields are: status, system, test level, priority and date

Example:
ID/Name: *N10 Compile a new risk report for a company in the road haulage industry.*
Status: *Cleared for testing*
Level: *System test*
Purpose of the Test Case
Here, you write a summary of the purpose of the test case.
Purpose: *Create a job with a new risk on an existing corporate customer with a good rating. The customer has not paid any interest or instalments against their credit limit for two months, and has therefore ended up in our risk system.*

Assumptions
Here, you define which assumptions apply, aside from the test data. It may, for example, be a question of other test cases or batches having to be run, or a particular system date.
Assumptions: *System date must be the 1st Quarter in 2028 when this test case is run*

Test Data
Here, you define the data which must be present for you to be able to execute the test case. It may be a matter of data in the system you are testing right now, and data in the system with which this system is communicating. You may choose to describe the test data in a document separately from the test case. In this case, you can reuse the same test case several times. It is common to generate the test cases first, and then fill it out with appropriate test data afterwards. Here, you should be careful which test data you are writing down, in order that it may be usable during regression testing in the future. For example, instead of writing a

particular personal identification number, you can write age and gender, and a particular date can be written relative to today's date, and so on.

Example:

General: *The customer must be a company and registered as a road haulage contractor, and have at least two registered agreements (loans). The test data are in a separate document.*

Specific: *Use customer 556778-4003 Last Rest Inc..*

Test Steps

Describe step by step the different sub processes in the test case. The level of each step may vary depending on which type of test is being run. It is important to remember to make it as practically useful as possible. An appropriate way of thinking is to do the same thing as in use cases, namely, to have one step for each thing you are carrying out, and a result which is then verified. The degree of detail is well suited for acceptance testing, where a limited number of test cases are run.

Results

You can verify certain things after each individual step, others after the whole test case has been run. It is important to describe all expected results before you carry out the tests – how else will you know whether it is correct or not? Both the output data and the system's state should be described. You can verify a test case in many different ways, by reports, windows in the application and database tools are among these ways.

For the most part, it is a good idea to compile the expected result when there is a risk of interpretation errors if you compile the answers in parallel with the execution of the tests. During exploratory testing, for example, it is not possible to develop the answers in advance, but this places heavy requirements on the observation skills of the person carrying out the tests.

22.1.3 Example of a Test Case for System and Acceptance testing

ID	N10 Set up new risk company				
Purpose	Create a job with a new risk on an existing corporate customer with a good rating. The customer has not paid any interest or instalments against their credit limit for two months, and has therefore ended up in our risk system.				
System	DEKT	Status		Author	TORY01
	The customer must be a company. System date must be the 1st Quarter in 2028 when this test case is run. Date must be 11th March at the latest				
Test Data	Customer 556778 - 4003 AB Sista Vilan				
Step	Description		Expected result		
1	Create new job		You come to the New job dialogue		
2	Type in the following data: Customer No. Customer since 1997, Nature of Business: Funeral Director, Cause of problem: Nobody is dying, Mark Account 583376258 + Others				
3	Fill in capital data: 1796, Security Pi 1796/1706 100%, Estimated risk 1500, + Transfer to obligation		Back to the obligation picture. Agreement updated.		
4	Note cause of report: New risk and period report. Cause: mark complete + OK		Job saved. You are back at the list of current jobs.		
Results checked after all steps are carried out					
1	Verify that the job is shown correctly in the list of current jobs.		Status: clear for acceptance, cause of report: P, N, date: today		
2	Verify that the job is shown correctly in the display: search by status: clear for acceptance and cause of report: period report		Status: clear for acceptance, cause of report: P, N, date: today		

Figure 22.2 Example of a test case description for system and acceptance testing. At this level, it may be appropriate to have relatively detailed instructions as to what has to be filled in, so that external resources can help with the execution.

22.1.4 Benefits and Drawbacks of Documenting in Such Detail

One of the weaknesses with testing is that no method is best suited to all situations.

Benefits of describing each detail in the test case are:
- It can be saved as a regression test case
- It requires less knowledge of the system as a whole
- A person from outside can carry it out with a little support
- You end up with documentation about your work, if this is needed
- The execution of the test case goes more quickly when you have decided on the details in advance.

Drawbacks of having overly detailed test cases may be that:
- When you are about to run the test case, you discover that the system has been changed, and that the details no longer match
- After having run a number of test cases, you have so much knowledge that you are no longer reading what is in the description and, therefore, risk making mistakes by missing certain details
- It takes ages longer to write down the details, time you could have used for designing more test cases, or carrying out tests

22.2 Test Chains
After the simple functions have been verified, you must also verify that the whole application fits together, including its manual routines. In this case, it often gets far too complicated and impractical to write everything in one single test case. You can link up several test cases in chains. Thus, a test chain consists of a number of test cases which are run in a particular sequence. It is like a red line running through the system during a particular period of time. It is appropriate to split up the test case into a chain if several different people are to carry out different parts, if we have to change the date in the system between different steps, or if completely different dialogues/functions in the system are used for different steps.

Test chains are especially well suited to verifying business processes, larger use cases, scenarios and during data and business cycle testing.

22.2.1 Components
Administrative Fields
Even for test chains, it is a good idea to have several administrative fields. A unique identifier is the most important one.

Example: N1 New-risk company

Purpose of the Test Chain
Here, you write down the overarching description of the purpose of the test chain.

Purpose: *The overarching purpose is to study the life cycle of a job from when it is created to when it is completed. An existing corporate customer with a good rating is not paying interest or instalments on their loan. A new job is then created with a new risk and, at the same time, a periodic report. The job is reviewed quarterly, with rising and falling risks, and is completed when the customer repays in full and changes bank – closing all its accounts.*

Test Data

Here, you define the data which must be present for you to be able to execute the test case. It may be a matter of data in the system you are testing right now, and data in the system with which this system is communicating. Often, you have developed specific test data for this very test case, and this is then specified here.

Test Data: The customer must be a company. Use customer 556778-4003 Last Rest Inc. continuously throughout the test case. The customer is reported by office 16983-2 which is in region 8.

Assumptions

Here, you define which assumptions apply, aside from the test data. For example, it may be a question of other test cases or batches having to be run, or a particular system date.

Assumptions: The tests begin in the Quarter 1 in 2028 and end in the Quarter 1 in 2029.

Test Cases

There have to be operators and an office manager in office 16983-8.
There has to be a regional manager for region 8.
Operators at central level are not included in this scenario.
Here, you make a list of the test cases included in the test chain, and in which order they are run.

The whole chain:
Q1 2028
Test Case: N10 New-risk company
Test Case: N11 Approve periodic report Q1 2028

Q2 2028
Test Case: N12 Risk worsens to likely loss
Test Case: N13 Approve periodic report Q2 2028

Q3 2028
Test Case: N14 Likely loss at repayment
Test Case: N13 Approve periodic report Q3 2028

Q4 2028
Test Case: N15 Job completed when customer pays all debts and changes bank
Test Case: N16 Approve periodic report Q4 2028

Q1 2029
Test case: N17 Verify job's status in the system after year end

22.2.2 Results
If you want to perform specific checks on the whole test chain, you fill in the points to check here. Many of the verifications, however, are performed in parallel with each individual test case.

22.2.3 How Large is a Test Chain?
A test chain can be seen as a red line running through the system. How long the line is, and what it contains, varies depending on the system. Some typical examples of how you can arrive at a test chain are time cycles and business processes.

22.3 Test Packages
A package contains test cases which are practical or necessary to run at the same time. When you write down your execution plan, you often write down which test packages are run each day. Often, it is not practically possible to run all test cases in a chain at the same time – this may require batches, rolling dates or something else amongst different parts.

22.3.1 Components
ID
Name the test package with a unique identifier in a way that is easy to understand.

Package:
Test Chains Q1 2028 (contains all test cases run in Quarter 1. This is practical when reports are compiled quarterly. For each quarter, approval occurs and special batch programs are run.)

Contents

Test packages are a way of grouping test cases you have to or should run at a particular point in time, at the same time or in a particular sequence. There is a clear advantage to setting up all test cases to be run on the same day in the same test package – it then becomes easier to administer and carry out the tests. Test packages may be split up, for example, by date. You must decide for yourself what suits your own project.

For verifying the business processes in the project, we created five test packages. East test package contained all the test cases run in a particular quarter for all business processes.

Test chains Q1 2028
Test chains Q2 2028
Test chains Q3 2028
Test chains Q4 2028
Test chains Q1 2029

22.3.2 How Do You Know What is a Good Test Package?

Again, this is a question of what is practical in your case. In the example above, we packaged by date. This is often, but not always, a good form of subdivision. At earlier levels of a project, you may choose to package by test area (function, dialogue, object etc.). A package may then contain, for example, a walkthrough of all the help texts in the system, or all the detail tests of a special window.

22.4 Execution Plan

In order to plan the execution of the tests in detail, you may create an execution plan for each test level. This contains information about who has to do what, and at what point in time.

22.4.1 Contents

Preparation

Usually, the level begins with preparation, e.g. loading base data, setting parameters, verifying the test environment. When you have succeeded in carrying out the preparations correctly, it is recommended that you perform a backup of the situation. Subsequent tests then begin from the backup and you avoid having to do the preparations several times. If changes occur which affect the preparatory activity, obviously, you must find out if it is necessary to regression test the preparations.

Happy-Day Testing

In order to check whether the application is ready to test, you often run some simple introductory tests. *Happy-Day* tests, as they are often called, are an introductory check on whether the system fits together. Use the central functions with simple data. Here, there is often a point of decision which says that you do not continue with any more tests before the most elementary ones are successful. You perform these introductory tests, appropriately, with each new larger delivery.

It can be regarded as curious that this is also called *Smoke Testing*, which stems from the good old days when we had to check circuit boards, which, with any defect in construction, could start to burn, giving off smoke as a result.

The Next Step

Subsequent tests can be split up in many different ways. For earlier levels, it is common, firstly, to verify individual dialogues, functions or test areas in detail, before you continue with more overarching scenario based tests.

Schedules are built according to what is most practical. Parameters affecting this are:

- the priority of the test area – the most important is tested first
- the order of delivery – this may differ from the priority of the tests
- the flow through the system may require particular functions to be carried out before others – the business processes are an important source of information
- time cycles govern which test dates apply

A common approach is, firstly, to make sure that the elementary tests are performed for the whole system, before you begin with test chains for the most important parts.

22.4.2 Example of an Execution Plan Overview

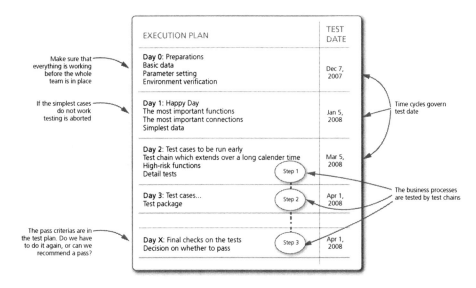

Figure 22.3: Execution plan overview for test level. It makes things easier to have some form of overview plan, especially if we are dependent on other systems and resources.

22.4.3 Example of an Execution Plan in Detail

Activity/test package	Time	Responsible	Comments
Day 1			
Verify test environment	16 oct	Leena	Check - list testchains.xls
Test Chains Q1 2028	17 oct	Torbjörn, Fredrik	
Point of decision	17.00	Leena	Clear to continue to Q2?
Day 2			
Test Chains Q2 2028	18 oct	Torbjörn, Fredrik	
Point of decision	17.00	Leena	Clear to continue to Q3?
Test Chains Q3 2028	19 oct	Torbjörn, Fredrik	
Point of decision	17.00	Leena	Clear to continue to Q4?
Day 4			
Test Chains Q4 2028	20 oct	Torbjörn, Fredrik	
Point of decision	17.00	Leena	Clear to continue to Q1 2029?
Day 5			
Test Chains Q1 2028	21 oct	Torbjörn, Fredrik	
Point of decision	15.00	Leena	Accept test chain or start again at Q1?

Figure 22.4: Execution plan of level of detail. As a test manager, I really want to be able to put in the plan who has to do what and when.

23 HANDLING DEFECTS

The purpose of writing a defect report is to get the defect fixed

- CEM KANER

THE BEST TESTER *is not the one who writes the most anomaly reports, but the one who have the most reports remedied*

Defects are regarded as all cases where the result of a test differs from what is expected. The cause of the defect is not always necessarily a program error. Other causes are interpretation of the requirement documentation or problems with the test cases. Defect, bug or incident are other terms used.

The chief purpose of creating a defect report is to have a defect you detect corrected. This makes the defect reports absolutely the most important thing you generate during the execution of tests. Handling defects is a central process, and it is important for it to work effectively. [106] Support with tools, and processes, can also be used for general job handling in a project, and with success, the database, along with test cases and defects, is taken over when handed over to the administration. There is much to be gained by continuing to build on the same ground for new releases of the system.

There are several reasons why it is interesting to have a standardised process for handling defects:[107]

- Control of all defects
- A shared working method makes for quicker handling
- To contribute toward creating a clear picture of the *status quo* and the quality of a version of a product
- To facilitate the review of projects
- A basis for continuous improvement
- To provide comparisons between different projects.
- To create common routines for statistics and reporting

23.1 Using Tools

If there is any area in which I actually recommend a tool, it is in handling defects. The time when we handled defects by unstructured mail, or in the form of documents in a folder, should be over now. There is a rich variety of tools, both commercial and free. Regardless of what you choose to rely on, make sure there is some kind of tool to facilitate your work. A small organisation does not need to buy the most expensive thing on the market, but can make do with a cheaper version which fulfils its purpose.

The benefits of using a tool which handles data centrally are, amongst other things, that:

- It saves time.
- Communication between parties improves and, regardless of where you are, there is a common way of handling defects, and you always see the right version.
- Analysis and reporting opportunities make it simple to develop a status report and prognosis quickly.
- Central prioritisation gives us focus on the right defects.
- It is easier to administer current jobs.
- The database's history makes for better analysis and opportunities for review.

23.2 The Work Process

It is important to adapt the work process so that it suits you. Sometimes, there may be a need for a very formal, detailed process, if many people are involved. In other cases, a detailed process is seen as a hindrance. Put simply, the life cycle of a defect can be split into four different steps.[108]

23.2.1 The Defect is Identified

Generate a report and document the steps for reproducing the defect. What is wrong and how serious it is. All information that facilitates further work is good – everything else is bad. Make a note of whether the defects occur irregularly, or cannot be recreated.

23.2.2 Analysis and Decisions About a Remedy

Analysis and prioritisation often occurs by means of a group assembled from project managers, test managers, development managers and, often, even those placing the order. The priority is the guiding force that the project team uses for determining what has to be corrected first. Keep the prioritisation list about acute remedies short, otherwise it will be ignored.

Here, it is a matter of having a smooth process in order not to hold up the work. Serious defects can be flushed out quickly to a responsible person, without the whole prioritisation group having to meet. The focus should be on the things which are unclear. How formally this is done can vary during the course of the project.

Decide whether the report is to be enacted, rejected without action, or dealt with at a later date. Appoint the responsible person.

23.2.3 Investigation and Action

The responsible person investigates the defect and finds out what the cause is. That responsibility remains until its remedy is executed, or the defect is delegated to another person. In smaller projects, it is more practical to discuss this with other project members than to ask a question via the report and change the person responsible. In larger projects, the opposite may be true.

23.2.4 Verifying the Correction

Before verification takes place, it is important to check that the correction of it is not only carried out, but that the new code is moved into the test environment. A good process for handling configuration prevents you from testing the wrong code. The tester who detected the defect, or the test manager, closes the report when it is verified. Consider which other test cases you should run in order to verify parts which may have been affected by the correction.

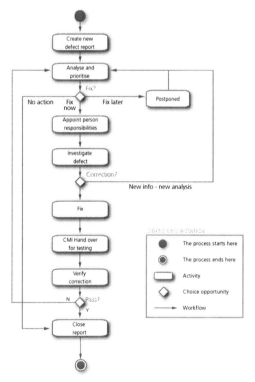

Figure 23.1: Suggestions for a work process for handling defects. Adapt the process to your local circumstances. Make it so simple that others follow it without great protest, but detailed enough in order to make for good control.

Adapt the process to your local circumstances. Make it so simple that others follow it without great protest, but detailed enough in order to make for good control.

23.3 Contents of the Defect Report
Important details to include are the following:

23.3.1 Title
Write something brief and relevant, so that you and all the other people involved can easily identify the report

23.3.2 Date Discovered/person
It is important to know who created the report and when it was done.

23.3.3 Person Responsible
There must always be someone who is responsible for the next step in handling the defect

23.3.4 Classification
How serious is the defect? Do not have too many classifications: three to five different levels is usually appropriate. One suggestion is as follows:

1. Critical – loss of data, security problems, a crash – the whole or large parts of the system are unusable if this defect remains. During testing – the tests cannot continue. During production – stops production.
2. Serious – stops functions, greater function errors without any opportunity for an alternative solution.
3. Minor – a minor function error or a serious error where there is an opportunity for an alternative solution.
4. Aesthetic defect – does not affect the functionality – spelling mistake, wrong colour or format.
5. Invalid – closed with no further action, not to be counted in the statistics (transpires after analysis)

23.3.5 Description of Defect
Write down the steps which must be taken to recreate the defect – it is very important to be extremely clear here. If you cannot recreate the defect yourself, how can the person who has to analyse the defect do it?

Isolation of the defect – if it is possible, it makes things much easier during later analysis if you can describe the specific situation where something goes wrong. It can be a matter of specific test data, a particular font, a combination of events, the first time you do something etc.

Certainly add an appendix with a screen-shot if this facilitates understanding.

23.3.6 Description of Remedy
This field is filled in during investigation/correction/testing and describes which changes have been made in order to fix the defect.

23.3.7 Priority
A supplementary field for directing the work. It is often set to *High*, *Normal* or *Low*. The difference from classification is that a defect may belong to a temporarily low-priority area, even if it is serious, and vice versa. Classification is an objective evaluation of a defect, and prioritisation, as way of choosing what is to be put right first.

23.3.8 Type of Defect
For us to have the opportunity of learning from our mistakes, it is necessary to analyse what it was that went wrong. We do this by an analysis of the causes of each report. A defect may depend on such widely differing things such as documentation, requirements, coding, design or testing.

23.3.9 Other Fields
Other interesting fields that can be used are, whether the defect is reproducible or not, which part of the system it lies in, test level, environment and version of the program code. In order to achieve smooth handling, it is important not to have too many fields to fill in, since the risk is that it becomes too heavy to handle. It is often best to use a simple process and relatively few fields.

23.4 Review
During the time where testing is under way, we can review the work done by measuring against test cases or by anomaly reporting. Information is used to give the project staff a picture of the current status, and is a basis for our decision to complete the tests.

In order to obtain an elementary status report on testing, I suggest two very simple diagrams to begin with.

I. The number of defects as per which week, which round of testing or which test level.
II. The number of test cases in total, run, successful or failed

23.4.1 Defects

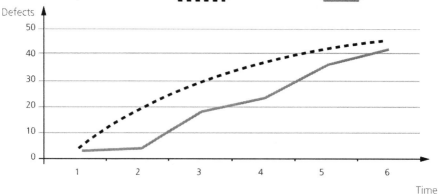

Summary of the total number (dashed line) and closed defects (solid line).

Figure 23.2: Summary of defects over time. The classic analysis of the diagram is that the tests begin to reach their conclusion when the total number of defects stops growing. This involves the upper curve levelling out. Moreover, the lower curve, which shows the number of closed defects, approaches the upper curve, which means that the defects detected have been corrected and verified.

The classic analysis of the diagram is that the tests begin to reach their conclusion when the total number of defects stops growing. This involves the upper curve levelling out. Moreover, the lower curve, which shows the number of closed defects, approaches the upper curve, which means that the defects detected have been corrected and verified. You get a more detailed picture by taking the classification of the defects into consideration. It is especially important to analyse the most serious defects carefully.

23.4.2 Number of Test Cases

Status of number of test cases run

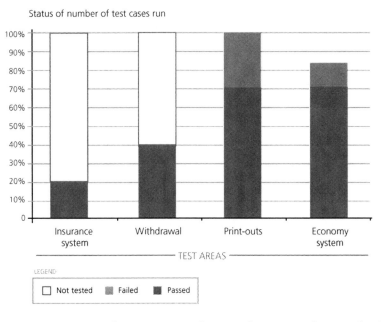

Figure 23.3: Summary of test cases and status by area. This graph shows how the project is proceeding, which areas are falling behind, and which are proceeding better.

Even here, there are a number of things to analyse. The total number of executed test cases, compared with the planned number, shows how much further we have to go with the execution. Both the number of failed test cases in itself, and in relation to the number of successful test cases, shows the quality of what has been delivered. A more detailed analysis takes which priority the test cases have into consideration, and how complicated they are.

23.4.3 Pitfalls

There is something fascinating in the simplicity of the diagram. At the same time, there are a number of obvious pitfalls. If we simply present a diagram of the number of defects, without relating it to the number of test cases, we do not know the reason why it looks the way it does. The fact that we are detecting fewer defects, or are succeeding in more test cases, may be down to us running fewer test cases, running the same test cases as before in order to verify corrections, or the area we are testing right now being simpler and, therefore, proportionally fewer defects being detected. It may also be down to us getting no new deliveries of code, or someone being off sick and, therefore, we have not continued to test on the same scope. Statistics can offer valuable information, but are not the ultimate truth. Moreover, invalid statistics can be directly damaging if they present a misleading picture of the situation.

It is very important that all diagrams you present are set in their context.

23.5 Subsequent Analysis

It is interesting, after a completed project, to analyse the test work with the aim of learning what we can do better next time. Some of the most important questions we can ask ourselves are:

- How did our compilation of tests work on a purely practical level?
- How was the aim fulfilled, of detecting serious defects at the start, and less serious ones towards the end?
- Did we detect the right type of defect at the right test level? If not, what was that down to?
- What were the causes of the defects we detected? Was it down to the requirements, design, coding, or factors in the testing process?
- In what ways can we do a better job next time?

Remarkably, there is often great resistance to analysing what went wrong. The cause of this may be a reluctance to change, or a suspicion that individual people have an accusing finger pointed at them. This is a shame, since we miss the chance to detect our weak points, and work on them in time for the next project.

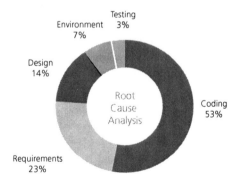

Figure 23.4: Analysis of causes of defects. It is interesting, after a completed project, to analyse the test work with the aim of learning what we can do better next time.

	Class 1 – Halts	Class 2 – Serious	Class 3 – Less serious	Class 4 – Aesthetic defect	Class 5 – Invalid	Sum for level	Total	Defect detection %
Unit integration test	2	6	0	0	2	8	111	7 %
System test	6	17	13	14	0	50	103	49 %
System integration test	3	12	1	2	0	18	53	34 %
Acceptance test	0	7	12	6	0	25	35	71 %
Production	0	5	1	4	0	10		
Total number of detected defects						111		

Figure 23.5 Table of defect discovery for different test levels. It is interesting to see how many defects sneak through each test level, especially since, on average, this costs more, the more defects that are discovered. We can never achieve 100% defect coverage in each level, but we can certainly get better and thereby earn more money.

Analysis of how many defects we have detected per test level produces a figure for the percentage of defects discovered. We detect how many of the defects remain at a given point in time in each test level. Since it is generally more expensive to detect and correct defects, the later they are discovered, we want a high percentage at each level. It is especially interesting to count the number of defect detected for the project as a whole. You can do this, by waiting until a certain period into the production stage, either a matter of months or before the next release, and counting up how many defects have occurred – this is called DDP – Defect Detection Percentage. For our example, this is:

$$\frac{\text{Total number of defects in testing}}{\text{Total number of defects in testing plus six months of production}} = \frac{8 + 50 + 18 + 25}{8 + 50 + 18 + 25 + 10} = 91\%$$

Figure 23.6: Calculation of percentage defects discovered for our work before production. Since we detect ten more defects in the first six months after the system has been tested, this clearly means that we have discovered 101 out of 111 defects, which is 91%. A fairer calculation also takes the classification of the degree of severity into account as a parameter.

A measurable aim for improvement might be to reduce the number of defects sneaking through into production, so that the percentage of defects discovered rises to 95%. Even here, it can be interesting to take into account how serious the defects are in our calculations, by simply counting serious defects or by weighting them differently.

FOOTNOTES
[106] Black, Rex[1999]: *Managing the Testing Process*
[107] Black, Rex[1999]: *Managing the Testing Process* pp. 107–111
[108] *IEEE 1044 Standard for Incidents*

24 WHEN CAN WE STOP TESTING?

THERE IS NO simple way of deciding when a system is completely tested. Most authors agree that there is no single criterion we can use in order to decide that we have finished the job. Here are some variants of opinion.

24.1 Five Criteria for Completion of Testing

According to Lee Copeland, there are five elementary criteria which, together, are usually used for decided when you can stop testing.[109] These are when:

1. We have achieved the coverage aims we defined in the strategy
2. The number defects discovered is lower than the boundary value we defined
3. The cost of detecting more defects is larger than the estimated loss arising from remaining defects.
4. The project team draws the collective conclusion that the product is ready to be released.
5. The decision maker gives the order to go to production.

There is a multitude of weaknesses in these criteria when taken one at a time. Glenford Myers suggests that the aim of reaching a certain level of coverage may run the risk of driving the testers towards writing fewer or inferior test cases, simply in order to manage running everything.[110] Not discovering any more defects may be down to us not testing in the right way, or the best testers being on holiday, but it does not necessarily mean that there are no more defects. The cost being more than the benefit of more test cases is a highly subjective evaluation which the tester is certainly not qualified to make: this is more a business issue. The consensus of the team may be a relatively better measure since, here, we discuss matters with developers, testers and people familiar with the operation together. The last criterion is a deadline which is decided outside the testers' domain, and actually has nothing to do with how well we have tested, but rather builds on a pure business judgement that we have to release the product by a certain date. It is common for many of the criteria above to be used in order to define collectively the criterion for finishing testing.

24.2 Good-Enough Quality

James Bach describes an approach he calls *Good-Enough Quality*, which he summarises with the following four points which must all be fulfilled.[111] Something is of good-enough quality if:

1. It has enough benefits
2. It has no critical problems

3. The benefits sufficiently outweigh the drawbacks
4. In the situation at hand, with all things considered, further testing and improvements would do more harm than good.

To arrive at the above, we can explain each part in a little more detail. Ask the following questions:
1. Which specific advantages does our product have? How great is the likelihood that one of our target customers will make use of a particular advantage? How important is each advantage? Which parts are critical? Are all advantages good enough for our target customers when taken together?
2. What potential problems does our product have? How great is the likelihood that one of our target customers will be exposed to a particular problem? How damaging can each problem be? What problems are wholly unacceptable? Are all problems, when considered together, too many for our target customers to be satisfied?
3. Does the product have enough advantages so that the drawbacks that happen to arise are few enough? How good does the product have to be in order to be accepted by the customers?
4. In what ways could we improve the product? What would this mean for our costs? Is there the possibility of delivering now, and then delivering improvements later? Precisely what advantages would we get from improving it? What problems could we have if we went on working, e.g. destroying what works, taking resources from other projects?

The conclusion of the regime above is that we have to use several different criteria together in order to achieve a good result. Moreover, it is most often not the testers who decide whether something is released. We provide information as to what we have achieved through our work, and leave it to the project manager or management group to make the decision to release. On the other hand, as a tester, you will certainly get asked the question: what do you think of the quality? Then, it is best for you to have an answer which is well founded.

FOOTNOTES

[109] Copeland, Lee [2003]: *A Practitioner's Guide to Software Test Design* p. 236
[110] Myers, Glenford [1979] *The Art of Software Testing*, pp. 122–128
[111] Bach, James[1997]: *Good Enough Quality: Beyond the Buzzword, Computer,* 8/97

25 SUGGESTED SOLUTIONS TO EXERCISES

25.1 Equivalence Partitions

In this case, I have concluded, by discussion with the requirement assessors, that the means of withdrawal should be chosen from a list (drop-down menu), therefore there are only four values to test. Other fields are filled in manually, and have a number of elementary format error controls.

Although I assume that the component test has been run on maximum/minimum and invalid values, I still perform a number of spot tests on the system. Testing all invalid values would take much more time: this should already be complete! The list below is what I consider a reasonable level for system test cases.

Description			1	2	3	4	5	6	7
		Prio	1	2	2	2	2	2	3
Parameter	Groups and boundary values	Values							
Surname	Valid	a - z, A - Z	X						X
		å, ä, ö, Å, Ä, Ö		X					X
		de, af, double - barrelled with space			X				X
		hyphen, accents, foreign names such as O'Connor				X			
		1 - 20 characters	X			X			X
		1 character A - Ö (Å is listed as a surname in the telephone directory!) (min)		X					
		20 characters (max)			X				
	Invalid	empty field					X		
		> 20 characters						X	
		21 characters							
		a character which is an underscore							
		characters not permitted, e.g, numerals, @, %							
Form of withdrawal	Valid	Personal account	X			X	X	X	
		Bank account		X					X
		Withdrawal card			X				
	Invalid	No choice made							
Amount	Valid	1 - 999 999 999 (can you have spaces or full stops as dividers?	X			X	X	X	X
		1 (is there any higher boundary in the set of rules, e.g, 50 SEK?) (min)		X					
		999 999 999 (max)			X				
	Invalid	decimal number							
		non - numeric characters, e.g, letters, calculation operators							
		< 1							
		0							
Tax	Valid	0 - 100	X			X	X	X	X
		0		X					
		100			X				
	Invalid	> 100 %							
		< 0 %							
		decimal number							
		non - numerical characters							
		empty field							
		underscore							

Figure 25.1: Suggested solution for exercise on developing equivalence partitions. The list below is what I consider a reasonable level for system test cases. The final appearance is decided on the basis of your knowledge of the system's logic and in what detail you want to test.

25.2 State Graphs

This is how the solution for the alcohol lock may look. Note that only the valid routes are drawn. A complete graph also contains all the *invalid* events. So, from standby mode, there should be another arrow going back into the standby mode again in its present location – Turn key / nothing happens. If we have to be really detailed, we may wonder whether there should not be an extra mode where the lock is on and the key has been turned – before the key is turned back, you cannot blow. In the same way, the other states, for example, like *control* and *restricted mode* have arrows going back on themselves for the events turn key and blow.

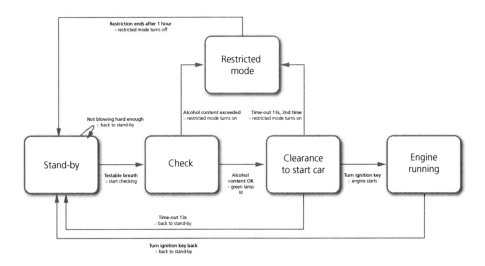

Figure 25.2: Suggested solution to state graph for the alcohol lock. Note that only the valid routes are drawn in order to prevent the graph from becoming too detailed. A complete graph also contains all the invalid events. Regardless of whether they are drawn up or not, they have to be tested.

No.	Start	Event	Answer	End
1	Stand - by	Breath test ok	Continue to check on exhaled air	Check
2	Stand - by	Not blowing hard enough	Back to stand - by	Stand - by
3	Check	Alcohol test shows alcohol content too high	Red lamp comes on. Restriction mode timer is set to 1 H	Restriction mode
4	Check	Alcohol test passed	Green lamp comes on. Ignition window open.	Authorisation to start car
5	Check	Time - out 13 s	Back to stand - by. Register failed ignition attempt	Stand - by
6	Check	Turn ignition key	The engine starts	Engine is running
7	Allowed to start engine	Time - out 13 s second time in a row	Red lamp comes on. Restriction mode timer is set to 1 H	Restriction mode
8	Engine is running	Turn ignition key back	Engine stops.	Stand - by
9	Restriction mode	Timer for restriction turns of after 1 hour.	Standby mode again	Stand - by

Figure 25.3: Suggested solution to table overview of transitions for the alcohol lock. We note in detail what leads to each transition and how the system responds. This is important information for our tests and, at the same time, is a form of quality assurance for the requirements.

In this case, the model is quite small. Therefore, it is also appropriate to draw a table for the transition pairings and make sure to cover in all the pairings with the test cases.

The next page shows a table of transition pairings, and the subsequent three test cases cover most of the rows in it. Another test case is needed to cover the last rows 7, 11 and 13.

Remember that each base test case is run several times in order to test both normal values and boundary values!

No.	Start	Step 1	Step 2
1	Stand - by	Stand - by	Stand - by
2	Stand - by	Stand - by	Check
3	Stand - by	Check	Authorisation to start car
4	Stand - by	Check	Restriction
5	Check	Authorisation to start car	Engine is running
6	Check	Authorisation to start car	Stand - by
7	Check	Authorisation to start car	Restriction
8	Authorisation to start car	Engine is running	Stand - by
9	Authorisation to start car	Stand - by	Stand - by
10	Authorisation to start car	Stand - by	Check
11	Authorisation to start car	Restriction	Stand - by
12	Check	Restriction	Stand - by
13	Restriction	Stand - by	Stand - by
14	Restriction	Stand - by	Check
15	Engine is running	Stand - by	Stand - by
16	Engine is running	Stand - by	Check

Figure 25.4: Suggested solution to table overview of transition pairings for the alcohol lock. Testing all the transition pairings makes for deeper testing of the system and helps us to detect defects that are dependent on combinations of transitions.

Base Test Case 1 – Happy Day
Assumption: You are in standby mode, you are sober

Execution:
1. Try to start the car without blowing
2. The attempt fails
3. Blow hard enough

4. Breath testing occurs
5. You get a green lamp and can turn the key
6. Start the car by turning the key within 15 seconds
7. Stop the engine by turning the key back
8. Verify that the engine is off by trying to start the car without blowing

Result/end state:
You have started and driven the car with a successful result. It is now in standby mode again.

Test coverage: this test case covers rows 3, 5 and 8

Base Test Case 2 – Happy Night?
Assumption: You are in standby mode and are extremely drunk.

Execution:
1. Blow hard enough
2. Breath testing occurs
3. You get a red light and a 1 hour block
4. After an hour, the block is taken off
5. Blow again, still drunk
6. Breath testing occurs
7. You get a red light and another 1 hour block
8. After an hour, the block is taken off and standby mode comes into play
9. Now, your friend, who is sober, blows
10. Breath testing occurs
11. You get a green lamp and can turn the key
12. However, your friend gets it wrong and the time-out is a factor – are you going to have to stay out all night?
13. Standby mode again
14. Now, your sober friend blows once again
15. Breath testing occurs
16. You get a green lamp and can turn the key
17. This time, your friend turns the key within 15 seconds
18. The engine starts
19. After having parked safely back home, the key is turned back
20. The engine stops
21. Your wife/husband is wondering what is going on and you really want to show them. Take a swig of whisky and blow again

ESSENTIAL SOFTWARE TEST DESIGN

22. Breath is tested and you get a red lamp
23. The 1 hour ignition block kicks in again and you cannot start the car however much you try.

Test coverage: besides the rows already covered earlier, this test case covers rows 4, 6, 10, 12 and 14

Base test case 3: Bad breath
Assumption: the system is in standby mode and you are sober, but have bad lungs

Execution:
1. Blow too weakly
2. You are back in standby mode
   H-10.   Blow too weakly again
   H-11.   **You are still in standby mode**
   H-12.   **Blow hard enough**
   H-13.   **Breath is tested**
   H-14.   **Green lamp**
   H-15.   **Time-out, since you do not start in time**
   H-16.   **Blow again, but too weakly**
   H-17.   **Blow again and hard enough this time**
   H-18.   **Breath is tested**
   H-19.   **You get a green lamp**
   H-20.   **Start the car within 15 seconds**
   H-21.   **Engine is running**
   H-22.   **Turn of the engine**
   H-23.   **Standby mode again**
   H-24.   **Blow again, but too weakly**
   H-25.   **Standby mode again**

Test coverage: besides the rows already covered earlier, this test case covers rows 1, 2, 9 and 15

25.3 Use Cases

So, pretty hard to read use case, wasn't it. The main reason for keeping it this way was that I read this use case it as an example from a couple of use-case specialists that claimed it was pretty good. My experience with use-cases are that they are usually pretty poor!

We start by developing the activity diagram.

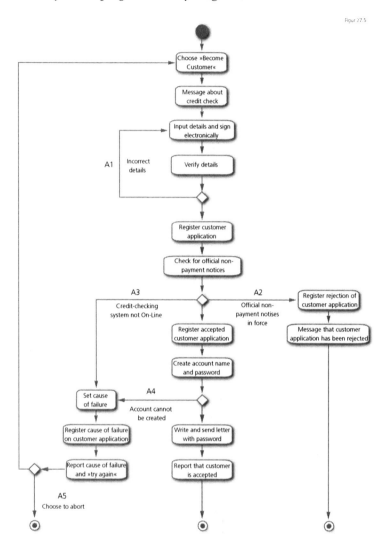

Figure 25.5: Suggested solution for activity diagram «Becoming a Customer of the Share Trading System». We have three different finishing points which all have different results. Only in one case has an account number been created. In the two other cases, the customer has either chosen to abort, or has been withheld from opening an account. For testing, it is even more important to mark clearly different results for alternative flows.

The operational variables are noted in a table

Scenario /TF - ID	Prio	Forename	Surname	Personal no.	Bank account no.	Electr. Signature	Customer system	Credit credit check	Expected result
Ha	1	Eva	Marklund	651212 - ####	######	OK	Customer exists,	No official non - payment notices,	Account name, password and user profile = > OK
/H - 001					Salary account		On - line	On - line	
Hb	1	Johan	Nilsson	780506 - ####	######	OK	Customer exists,	No official non - payment notices,	Account name, password and user profile = > OK
/H - 002					Savings account		On - line	On - line	
A1a		Eva	Marklund	651212 - ####	######	OK	Customer exists,	No official non - payment notices,	Message that personal identification number is not correct.
/A1 - 001					Salary account		On - line	On - line	No user profile, account name or password is created.
A1b		Johan	Nilsson	780506 - ####	another person's account number	OK	Customer exists,	No official non - payment notices,	Message that the submitted account number does not belong to the Potential Customer
/A1 - 002							On - line	On - line	No user profile, account name or password is created.
A1c		Johan	Nilsson	780506 - ####	wrong account number	OK	Customer exists,	No official non - payment notices,	Message that account number is incorrect
/A1 - 003							On - line	On - line	No user profile, account name or password is created.
A1 - d		Johan	Nilsson	780506 - ####	######	Defect	Customer exists,	No official non - payment notices,	Message about defective electronic signature
/A1 - 004					Savings account		On - line	On - line	No user profile, account name or password is created.
A2		Christin	Andersson	740303 - ####	######	OK	Customer exists,	Official non - payment notices,	Message that application is aborted due to official non - payment notice
/A2 - 005					Salary account		On - line	On - line	No user profile, account name or password is created.
A3		Christin	Andersson	740303 - ####	######	OK	Customer exists,	NO	Message that application can not be dealt with at the moment.
/A3 - 006					Salary account		On - line	On - line	No user profile, account name or password is created.

Figure 25.6, on the previous page: Suggested solution for operational variables «Become a Customer» We have chosen to include all variables calculated in the use case, even though it can be debated whether they are all «governing».

When the variables affecting the expected result of the flow come up in the tables, and scenarios begin to take shape, a number of unanswered questions arise, as well as considerations as to whether what is described is correctly thought out. Here are some examples of questions which arose when we developed activity diagrams and operational variables:

- Why are Name, personal ID number etc. operational variables? Should the system not already have these, since the customer has to be logged in on their internet banking system to be able to make an application? Uncertain assumptions.
- Can the Potential Customer abort only at steps A3–4 and A4–4?
- If the account number cannot be created, what does the Share Trading System do with the registered and approved customer application? For the customer's sake, it should surely be saved so that we can inform of the result later.
- If the account number already exists, how is the Share Trading System to react?
- If the customer system is not on-line, how can the Potential Customer be verified?
- How far back in time must the Share Trading System take into account as regards any non-payment notices?
- If we perform a credit check every time the customer applies, that implies that a customer applying again gives rise to an increased cost for us. (When it is a matter of money, people react)

The questions are raised together with those setting the requirements and, afterwards, the requirements are reviewed with clarifications and changes.

We have picked out the following suggestions for one of the base test cases.

ID	Base test case H Become Customer - Create user profile, account name and password				
Purpose	Create a user profile with account name and password for a user which has previously been a customer of the bank				
System	SHARE	Status		Mailouts	Actor	Potential Customer
Author	ANBO26	Priority		High		
Test level	ST/AT	Date		38526		
	The Potential Customer is already a Customer of the bank, with a live account				
	The Potential Customer is logged in to the internet banking system				
	The Share Trading System is up				
	The Customer System is up				
	The Credit Checking System is up				
	There are no liability orders				
Test Data	See the table governing variable for UC Become Customer.				
	Current Scenario/Test case: Ha/H001 & Hb/H002				
Step	Description		Expected result		
1.	Choose to »Become Customer«		Window shown for registering personal information		
2.	Register forename, surname, personal identification number and bank account. Choose to send details.		Dialogue shown for electronically signing the customer application.		
3.	Register current electronic signature. Choose to continue		The Dialogue is closed and a window is shown with information that the application is being dealt with.		
4.	-		When the application has been accepted by the Share Trading System, a new window is shown with information that the application is accepted, account name has been set up, and the password is being sent by letter.		
5.	Choose »Start page«		Window with the Internet banking system's first page is shown		
Results checked after all steps are carried out					
1.	Check that the account name has been created for the Customer				
2.	Check that the right bank account is linked to the account name				
3.	Ensure that an output data file has been generated containing the Customer's password		The output data format is verified in another test case		
4.	Check that it is possible to log in on the Share Trading System with the password generated		Password is generated via the test support application		

Figure 25.7: A base test case for «Becoming a Customer of the Share Trading System». We have chosen the Main flow and described the test case in detail, so that a member of the operations staff can take part in its execution with a little support.

25.4 Decision Table

I detect six rules slipped into the field description, and these are written down in the table.

I choose to test each rule by leaving one mandatory field blank at a time. This is relatively quick to run since it is a dialogue giving me a direct connection. For rule 3, for example, I would fill in Eurobond as an instrument class, and then leave Financial Group empty but Clearing Mode and Account filled in. The next step is to fill in Financial Group but delete Clearing Mode and so on. In this way, I check that the field control is working for one field at a time.

Field Name	Value Set	Rule0	Rule1	Rule2	Rule3	Rule4	Rule5
Name on card	Read only						
Customer number	Read only						
Fi - group	01, 02, 03	Mandatory	01	Mandatory	Mandatory	Mandatory	Mandatory
Clearing mode	KASS, CEDE, EUCL		Mandatory	Mandatory	Mandatory	Mandatory	Mandatory
Instrument class	Eurobond, blank			Eurobond			
Business type	AVM, BSP, DEP, EMU, DFO				Business type filled in	Mandatory	Mandatory
Country	Country code std					Country code filled in	Mandatory
Currency	Currency code std						Currency code filled in
Account	Euroclear, Kassevere, Cedel	Mandatory	Mandatory	Mandatory	Mandatory	Mandatory	Mandatory

Figure 25.8: Suggested solution for decision table for field control. I detect six rules slipped into the field description, and these are written down in the table. I choose to test each rule by leaving one mandatory field empty at a time

25.5 Decision Tree

TIP: Write in the set of rules in Excel and hide rows and columns as they are written into the tree.

1. The first condition of the tree is the error handling found in rule 21.

2. The next subdivision was performed on the issue of whether the person was a home-owner or not: this parameter was present in all the rules left when rule 21 had disappeared.
3. For those who were home-owners, the next parameter was whether there were any official non-payment notices or not.
4. The next parameter was capital loss, and so on.
5. Since the set of rules is complex, we can either split up certain rules into several different leaves, or take up the capital loss parameter in several places on the tree. This leads to rules 7 and 13 appearing in several leaves in solution 1. One rule is missing in the condition *Factor Increase in Income in Previous Year <=1.2*

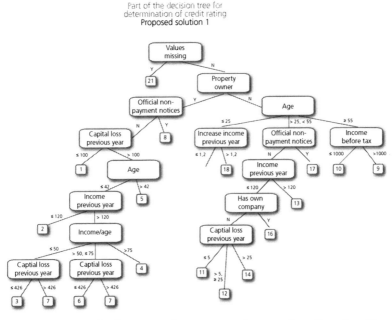

Figure 25.9: Suggested solution 1, decision tree for set of credit rules. Since the set of rules is complex, we can either split up certain rules into several different leaves, or take up the capital loss parameter in several places on the tree. This leads to rules 7 and 13 appearing in several leaves in solution 1.

Suggested solution 2
Here, we have given the tree more depth by including the same parameter several times instead. Thus, we end up with fewer leaves. This implies that we end up with fewer test cases. Here, we have added the missing rule with a question mark instead of a rule number.

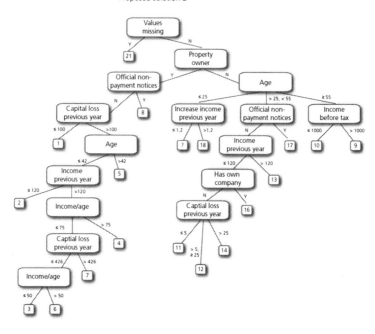

Part of the decision tree for
determination of credit rating
Proposed solution 2

Figure 25.10: Suggested solution 2, decision tree for a set of credit rules. Here, we give the tree more depth by including the same parameter several times instead. Thus, we end up with fewer leaves. This implies that we end up with fewer test cases. Here, we have added the missing rule with a question mark instead of a rule number.

The test cases are then built from the tree.
In order to test each leaf, we set up at least two test cases, a normal value and a boundary value. How many are required depends on how the code looks. In the actual project, 2–4 test cases per rule are used in order to achieve good coverage.

Test cases where some value is missing are tested in rule 21. You can read more about how many test cases you should have in the next technique, elementary comparisons – this says that every included variable must have the opportunity to be decisive at some point. In our case, this means that each value involved in the error handling system should be missing, one at a time, while the others are present.

The test data are then created, with one row in the data file for each test case. The key is that the test case must find the right rule and that the correct rating 1–5 is assigned.

25.6 Elementary Comparison

25.6.1 Suggested Solution

	Description	Test Case 1	Test Case 2	Test Case 3	Test Case 4	Test Case 5
R1.1 (0)	Age ≥18	X		X	X	X
R1.2 (1)	Age < 18		X			
R2.1 (0 1 1)	Age > 40 is false, so the rule is false		X			
R2.2 (1 0 1)	Salary < 20k is false, so the rule is false.	X				
R2.3 (1 1 0)	No liability orders is false, so the rule is false			X		
R2.4 (1 1 1)	All conditions true, so the rule is true				X	X
R3.1 (1 0 0 0)	Gold membership means an extra charge of 500 is added	X				
R3.2 (0 1 0 0)	Elite Player means an extra charge of 500 is added		X			
R3.3 (0 0 1 0)	Ball subscription means an extra charge of 500 is added			X		
R3.4 (0 0 0 1)	Racket Service means an extra charge of 500 is added				X	
R3.5 (0 0 0 0)	No special values give 0 as a change					X
	Fee	2500	500	2500	2000	1500

Figure 25.11: Suggested solution for elementary comparisons. Four variables gives us 4+1 test cases if we firstly test one variable at a time as true, and finally all the variables as simultaneously false. We can combine the test conditions with already existing test cases where the rules are mutually independent.

25.6.2 Discussion About a Test Case Which Fails to Appear

In this case, we skip over the condition where a member has several of the conditions elite player, gold member, ball subscription or racket service, since these have each already determined that 500 is added to the fee. However, what happens if the developer interprets the requirement as elite player and gold member each implying 500 kronor extra in their own right? We miss this defect if we skip the test case. Or, perhaps, is it supposed to be that way, and is the requirement therefore wrong?

Remember that the technique is only a form of guidance, and only detects certain types of defect. Techniques are good to have, but it is your knowledge which is decisive as to how good the tests are!

25.7 Combinatorial Testing

1)

The input parameter model contains three parameters (A, B, and C). This results in three possible parameter pairs (<A,B>, <A,C>, and <B,C>). To achieve 100% 2-wise coverage every possible combination of values of each parameter pair should be included in at least one combination. With each parameter having four values, there are 16 possible combinations of values (<1,1>,<1,2>, <1,3>, <1,4>, <2,1>,... ,<4,4>) of each pair of parameters. This gives a total of $3*16 = 48$ value pairs.

- The set of 9 combinations in Figure 7 that satisfy 2-wise valid coverage cover 27 of the 48 possible pairs => $27/48 = 56.25\%$ 2-wise coverage.

- The set of 13 combinations in Figure 9 that satisfy base choice coverage cover 21 of the 48 possible pairs => $21/48 = 43.75\%$ 2-wise coverage.

26 GLOSSARY

Attack Pattern
James Whittaker's contribution to how we develop good test cases. Technical focus.

Defect
A test result which differs from what is expected.

Black Box test
We regard the system as a black box and concern ourselves only with input and output data, and not with precisely what is happening within the system.

Base test case
Test cases where we have not yet concerned ourselves with paying attention to the test data in detail.

Boolean algebra
A form of notation developed by the mathematician Boole as an aid to solving logical problems. Handles data sets and operations on these and logical operations. Specifically, the logical operators AND, OR and NOT which are the basis of all data processing.

Boundary values
We start from the equivalence partitions and test the values lying in the margin of each group, for example, maximum and minimum.

Component
A collection of code which realises a function.

Context-driven school
Alliance working from the assumption that all test efforts are dependent on context, and that there is no universal solution.

Dialogue
Graphical user interface where the user can interact directly with the system

Domain Testing
Equivalence partitioning where several variables cooperate, and therefore have to be tested together.

Equivalence partition
A grouping of data or test cases which are assumed to test the same things. The principle is that only one value in the same group needs to be tested.

Exploratory testing
Exploratory testing is, at the same time, learning, test design and test execution, as opposed to scripted testing.

Execution plan
A schedule describing how the tests are to be.

Happy Day Testing

A term for simple introductory tests. Also called smoke-testing and health check

Heuristics

A fallible method for solving a problem or making a decision. Heuristics are also called guidelines, suggestions, or rules of thumb.

ISTQB

The International Software Testing Qualifications Board, responsible for international terminology and certification.

Model

A simplification of an actual situation, for the purpose of helping us solve a problem.

Non-functional testing.

Collective concept for tests including parts which are not counted as direct functions, for example, usability, performance characteristics. Also called quality characteristics.

Oracle

The source which gives us the expected result of a test.

Persona

A precise description of the user, what he or she wants to achieve, and why. The method caters mostly for designers and architects, but is also useful for test design.

Popper, Karl

Appointed by me to be the testers' own philosopher. Author, amongst other things, of the book about the philosophy of science, *Conjectures and Refutations*. Popper describes how our knowledge of science grows through our exposure of our hypotheses to critical tests. In the same way, we testers expose the software to our own critical tests. We can never know for certain whether something is correct, but the more advanced tests we manage to carry out, the more certain we become that it works.

Requirement Analyst

Role found in certain development processes. Receives and analyses the requirements developed.

Scenario

Route through a use case.

Scripted testing

Tests which are carried out with the aid of previously written instructions: the opposite of exploratory testing.

Static testing

Carried out without the code being executed, for example, review or analysis of documentation or code.

Structural testing

The focus is on what happens in the code, the right challenge to the right table, important but not enough to cover all of the code with the tests.

Taxonomy

A way of classifying things by grouping them according to similar characteristics.

Technical tests

I use the term technical to emphasise that the tests lie nearer the code than the average user's interface.

Test case

A collection of instructions describing how a test is to be carried out.

Test chain

A sequence of consecutive test cases run in a particular order.

Test package

A way of practically gathering together test cases which, for example, are to be run simultaneously by the same person.

Unified Process

Abbreviated as UP, created by Ivar Jacobsson, a commercial variation is called RUP, where the R stands for the company Rational.

White Box test

See Structural testing.

27 SUGGESTED READING

27.1 Testing
Copeland, Lee : A Practitioner's Guide to Test Design
A thoroughly excellent book which goes through many of the most important elementary techniques of test design in detail. Easy to read with many good examples. The best book in English about test design

Gilb, Tom, Dorothy Graham: Software Inspection
A thorough walkthrough of review techniques for software development.

Kaner, Cem: Testing Computer Software
This book is marketed with the motto, «The best selling book on testing of all time». It is obvious that the authors have solid experience of testing. They have filled the book with a little of absolutely everything. In barely 500 pages, a broad spectrum of tests are described, from details about test design to error handling and test management. Buy it and keep it as a reference book, read a new section to get ideas.

Kaner, Cem, James Bach, Brett Petticord: Lessons Learned in Software Testing
293 tips on 263 pages, a mixture of shorter and slightly longer tips. The book builds entirely on the authors' own experiences. Reading it is like having a conversation with some of the world's best testers, and it is a source of inspiration for me in my work in testing. Do not look on every sentence as an absolute truth, but rather as an inspiration to new thinking. It is a good complement to your other reference literature, since this book questions many old truths. The book comes from the Context-Driven School, which works according to the fact that what is good is dependent on the situation at hand.

Kit, Edward: Software Testing in the Real World
A neat little book of 240 pages, dealing which improvement of the test process. It is easy to read and gives a good overview, starting from a variant of the V model called «The Dotted-U Model». The model stems from showing how each part of setting the requirements and development have a corresponding activity in testing. The book is well suited as an introduction for those of you who want to learn the basics of testing, but is also a good reference work for the more experienced tester. Recommended for your personal reference library.

Myers, Glenford [1979] The Art of Software Testing
This book, ground breaking at the time, was written as early as 1979. It has become something of a cult book, which is often referred to in more modern literature It is, in fact, hard to find a newer book about testing which DOES NOT make any reference to this one! A lot of what was written then is still as current, even if the presentation of it is a little thin compared with the rich variety of literature in the field which is about today. Brilliant to have, but needs to be supplemented with newer literature

TPI – Test Process Improvement
A must in every serious test specialist's bookcase. A practical description of how to improve the test process step by step. I personally keep it as a source of inspiration to the next activity in the company and, at the same time, my own education plan. The book contains a description of different test areas, and what has to be fulfilled in each area in order to achieve a particular level. On the other hand, it is no text book on the subject of testing.

Whittaker, James: How to Break Software
Practical tips for how to systematically detect the commonest defects in software. The focus is on robustness and the way of working builds on inclusive knowledge about development and programming language. Disturbingly few pages, not a lot of chatter but straight down the line on the techniques. Examples that are easy to follow.

Whittaker, James[2003]: How to Break Software Security
Like his other book, but the focus is on how to detect security problems in software.

27.2   Other Literature
27.2.1 Usability
Cooper, Alan: The Inmates Are Running the Asylum
Why the systems we build become so difficult to use. A book which everyone in software development, and those who commission IT systems, should read. Both amusing and important, and also easy to read.

Cooper, Alan: About Face 2.0
The basics of interaction design. How we obtain usable systems. A book which stands a chance of revolutionising our way of designing technical products.

Norman, Donald A: The Design of Everyday Things
An excellent description of why bad design makes users fail in their attempt to use a device from a door to an advanced technical product.

27.2.2 Requirement Handling and Process
Fowler, Martin, Kendall Scott :UML Distilled:
Introduction to the notation standard UML.

Kruchten, Philippe: Rational Unified Process
Introduction to RUP, now also in Swedish.

Leffingwell, Dean, Don Widrig: Managing Software
Requirements: A Use Case Driven Approach Requirement handling with use cases, one of the better books on the market.

Robertson, Suzanne, James Robertson [1999]: Mastering the Requirements Process
Requirement handling with use cases, also one of the better books on the market. Deals with the whole process.

Schneider, Geri, Jason Winters[2000]: Applying Use Cases
Introduction to use cases.

Weinberg, Gerald: Exploring Requirements: Quality Before Design
How we develop requirements with quality.

27.2.3 Philosophy, Psychology and Scientific Theory
de Bono, Edward: Lateral Thinking
Easy to read and brilliant on the subject of problem solving. Get better at thinking outside your usual boundaries, and perform more advanced test cases

Levy, David A: Tools of Critical Thinking
Worth thinking about, on the subject of traps in our way of thinking. Actually a text book for psychologists, but well worth reading.

Popper, Karl: Conjectures and Refutations
This work describes how science develops, as we firstly develop hypotheses and estimates, then expose them to critical tests to see if they stand up. The same procedure applies to software testing where, through developing really good

test cases, we can ensure that the final product maintains high quality. If you must read any philosopher, read Popper.

Weinberg, Gerald: An Introduction to General Systems Thinking
Useful book dealing with scientific theory. How we solve problems by building models and systematising

27.3 Internet Resources
www.howtobreaksoftware.com: Here you can download the latest versions of *Holodeck* and *Canned Heat*, which help you to simulate different problem situations for the testing of robustness.

www.model-based-testing.org: masses of links to interesting articles about models, and how they help us in testing. Special focus on formal models and automation.

www.satisfice.com: contains a large collection of articles worth reading, both to read and download. Read the latest about *Exploratory Testing* and download templates and free programs like *allpairs.exe*

www.pairwise.org: a collection of tools and articles on pairwise testing

www.context-driven-testing.com: Information about this modus operandi

27.4 Standards in Testing
The most widespread standards around today are listed below. Most of the documentation is in English.

- www.istqb.org: here you will find the standard for international certification, with links to the different countries' national versions.
- BS 7925-2:1998. Software Component Testing.
- DO-178B:1992. Software Considerations in Airborne Systems and Equipment Certification, Requirements and Technical Concepts for Aviation (RTCA SC167).
- IEEE 829:1998. Standard for Software Test Documentation.
- IEEE 1008:1993. Standard for Software Component testing.
- IEEE 1012:1986. Standard for Verification and Validation Plans
- IEEE 1028:1997. Standard for Software Reviews and Audits.
- IEEE 1044:1993. Standard Classification for Software defects.

- IEEE 1219:1998. Software Maintenance.
- ISO 9000:2000. Quality Management Systems – Fundamentals and Vocabulary.
- ISO/IEC 9126-1:2001. Software Engineering – Software Product Quality – Part 1: Quality characteristics and sub-characteristics.
- ISO/IEC 12207:1995. Information Technology – Software Life Cycle Processes.
- ISO/IEC 14598-1:1996. Information Technology – Software Product Evaluation - Part 1: General Overview

28 REFERENCES

Articles

Ammann, P. E. and Offutt, A. J. [1994]: Using Formal Methods to Derive Test Frames in Category Partition Testing, in Proceedings of Ninth Annual Conference on Computer Assurance (COMPASS'94), Gaithersburg MD, pp. 69–80, IEEE Computer Society Press, June 1994.

Bach, James [2005]: Rapid Testing course material.

Bach, James[2006]: Exploratory Testing Explained v 3.0

Boehm, B W [1976]: Software Engineering, IEEE Transactions on Computers, C-25

Chow, T.S. [1978]: Testing Software Design Modeled by Finite-State Machines, IEEE Transactions on Software Engineering 4

Cohen, D. M., Dalal, S. R., Kajla, A., and Patton, G. C. [1994]: The Automatic Efficient Test Generator (AETG) system, in Proceedings of Fifth International Symposium on Software Reliability Engineering (ISSRE94), Los Alamitos, CA, USA, Nov 6–9, 1994, pp. 303–309, IEEE Computer Society Press, Nov 1994

Fagan, Michael[1976]: Design and Code inspections to Reduce Defects in Program Development. IBS Systems Journal, 15(3)

Gardiner, Julie[2005]: EuroSTAR2005

Gross, J. and Yellen, J. [1998]: Graph Theory and its Applications

Grove Consultants [2002]: Test Practitioner course material

Herzlich, Paul [1993]: W-model, www.evolutif.co.uk/default.asp?page=services/wmodel.html

www.testingeducation.org/BBST/BBST--IntroductiontoTestDesign.html

Kaner, Cem [2005] groups.yahoo.com/group/software-testing/message/2880

Kwan, M-K. [1962] «Graphic Programming Using Odd and Even Points», Chinese Journal of Mathematics, Vol. 1

Lei, Y. and Tai, K. C. [1998]: In-Parameter-Order: A Test Generation Strategy for Pairwise Testing, in Proceedings of the Third IEEE High Assurance Systems Engineering Symposium, pp. 254–261, IEEE, Nov 1998

Mealy G.H. [1955] A Method for Synthesizing Sequential Circuits» Bell System Technical Journal 34 pp. 1045–1079

Moore E.F. «Gedanken Experiments on Sequential Machines In Automata Studies, Annals of Mathematical Studies No. 34 Princeton, NJ: Princeton University Press

Rapps S. and Weyuker E.J. [1985]: Selecting Software Test Data Using Dataflow Information,

IEEE Transactions on Software Engineering, SE-11(4), pp. 367–375, Apr 1985

Robinson, Harry: [2005]: EuroSTAR Tutorial

Robinson[2005]: EuroSTAR Tutorial Model-Based Testing

Robinsson Harry, Steven Rosaria [1999]: Applying Models in your Testing Process, Intelligent Search Test Group, Microsoft Corporation

Royce, Dr Winston [1970]: Managing the Development of Large Software Systems

Williams, A. W. and Probert, R. L. [1996]: A Practical Strategy for Testing Pair-wise Coverage of Network Interfaces, in Proceedings of Seventh International Symposium on Software Reliability Engineering (ISSRE96), White Plains, NY, USA, Oct 30 – Nov 2, 1996, pp. 246–254, IEEE Computer Society Press, Nov 1996.

www.context-driven-testing.com

Zimmerer, Peter[2005]: Eurostar presentation

Books and Reports

Beck, Kent [2003]: Test-Driven Development

Beizer, Boris[1995], Black Box Testing

Beizer, B. [1990]: Software Testing Techniques

Black, Rex[1999]: Managing the Testing Process

Cooper, Alan: About Face 2.0

Copeland, Lee: A Practitioner's Guide to Test Design

Fowler Martin, Kendall Scott [2003] :UML Distilled: A Brief Guide to the Standard Object Modeling Language (Object Technology S.)

Gilb, Tom, Dorothy Graham [1993]: Software Inspection

Grindal, M. [2007]: Handling Combinatorial Explosion in Software Testing, Linköping Studies in Science and Technology, Dissertation No. 1073, ISBN 978-91-85715-74-9.

IEEE Standard 610.12-1990

ISTQB course plan version 0.2. www.sstb.se

Kaner, Cem, Jack Falk, Hung Nguyen[1999]: Testing Computer Software

Kit. Ed[1995]: Software Testing in the Real World

Kruchten, Philippe [2002]: Rational Unified Process – En introduction

Leffingwell, Dean, Don Widrig[2003]:Managing Software Requirements: A Use Case Approach

McConnell, Steve [2004]: Code Complete The second edition

Myers, Glenford [1979] The Art of Software Testing

Pol, Martin, Ruud Teunissen, Erik van Veenendaal [2002] Software Testing – A Guide to the TMAP Approach

Robertson, Suzanne, James Robertson [1999]: Mastering the

Requirements Process

Schneider Geri, Jason Winters[2000]: Applying Use Cases

Schrage, M. (1996) Cultures of Prototyping in Winograd, T. [ed.] (1996) Bringing Design to Software (Chapter 10), New York: Addison-Wesley.

Weinberg, Gerald[1971]: The Psychology of Computer Programming

Weinberg, Gerald[2001]: An Introduction to General Systems Thinking, Chapter 1

Whittaker, James[2003]: How to Break Software

Whittaker, James[2003]: How to Break Software Security

29 INDEX

55–65, 67, 70–75, 80–81, 84, 95, 224, 261–262, 268, 271

Happy Day testing 262

Heuristics 15, 35, 60, 67, 73, 83, 262

Input data 28, 35, 108, 115, 165, 195, 205–206

Inspection 27, 54, 778, 89, 265, 271–272

Integration testing 50, 81

Istqb 42, 49, 56, 83, 89, 262, 268, 272

Kaner 23, 29, 31, 59, 71, 75, 84, 89, 157, 198, 209, 233, 265, 271–272

Mealy 139, 146, 157, 271

Model 15–16, 21–22, 24–25, 27–47, 53, 65, 6768, 77, 79, 82, 85, 93–94, 97–99, 117–119, 130, 139–140, 148–149, 159, 163, 165, 170, 177–186, 188, 191, 195, 197, 199, 201, 211, 248, 260, 262, 265, 268, 272

Moore 139, 145–146, 157, 271

Myers 31, 38, 89–90, 118, 209, 243–244, 266, 272

Node 139–140, 144–146

Oracle 33, 35, 37, 67, 262

Output data 81, 85, 101, 105, 115, 195, 205–206, 224, 261

Persona 19, 36, 75, 82, 98, 119, 136, 160–161, 195, 197, 224, 254, 262, 265–266

Popper 21, 27, 263, 267–268

Printer 108–109, 112

Priority 106, 223, 230, 234, 237, 239

Process 16, 21–23, 27, 33, 39–40, 44–47, 52, 55, 58–62, 64–65, 67, 69–70, 73–74, 79–81, 83–93, 101, 103, 108, 119, 121–124, 127, 135–140, 158, 165, 191, 193, 199, 203, 217, 222, 224, 226, 228–230,

233–237, 240, 242, 263, 265–267, 269, 272–273

Prototype 124–125

Q-pattern 206–207, 209

Quality factor 77, 82

Reports 64, 71–72, 80, 195–196, 224, 228, 233, 273

Requirement analyst 262

Requirements 21, 23, 27–29, 31, 35, 39–46, 51–55, 69, 73, 77, 82, 85–86, 93–94, 119, 121, 127, 136, 138, 147, 160, 164, 191, 195, 199, 201–204, 206–207, 224, 237, 240, 248, 254, 262, 264, 267–268, 272–273

Review 23–24, 27, 29, 41–44, 61, 64, 66, 68, 77–79, 127, 160, 198, 206–207, 209, 222, 227, 233–234, 237, 254, 262, 265, 268

Risk 39, 41, 43–45, 52–55, 59–60, 69–72, 75, 79–80, 83–84, 108, 111–112, 127, 131, 142, 153, 161, 164, 174, 201–206, 209, 223–224, 226–227, 237, 243

Robustness testing 35

RUP 27, 263, 267

Scenario 34, 63–64, 83–84, 95, 124–125, 127, 131–132, 134–136, 203, 226–227, 230, 254, 262

Scripted testing 53, 57, 59–62, 74, 261, 263

Software 17, 19, 21–23, 27, 31, 38–39, 45–47, 50, 55, 57–59, 61–62, 66–67, 72, 75, 82–83, 89–90, 125, 138, 157, 168, 175, 177, 188–189, 194, 198, 201, 205–207, 209, 217, 244, 262, 265–269, 271–273

Standard 21, 34, 38, 42, 49, 67, 71, 73–74, 77–78, 82–84, 130, 138,

E

Printed in the United Kingdom
by Lightning Source UK Ltd.
135811UK00002B/91/P

9 789185 699032